KT-452-680
May, 1963
With all good wishes

TRAVELLING TONGUES

TRAVELLING TONGUES

Debating Across America

by

KENNETH HARRIS

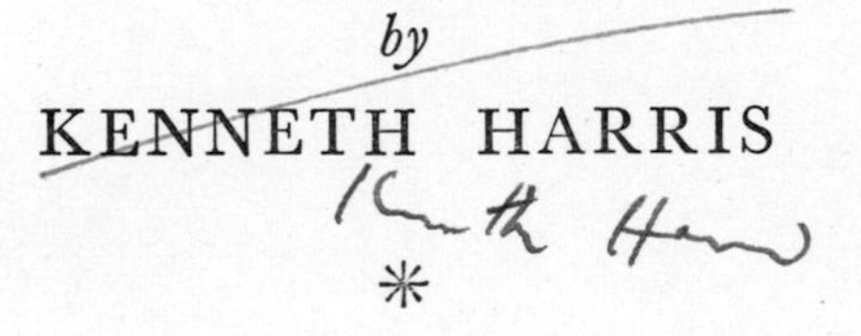

*

WITH A PREFACE BY

ARTHUR BRYANT, C.B.E., LL.D.

LONDON

JOHN MURRAY, ALBEMARLE STREET, W.

First Edition. . . November, 1949
Reprinted . . . January, 1950
Reprinted . . . March, 1950

Printed in Great Britain by
Wyman & Sons, Ltd., London, Fakenham and Reading

CONTENTS

		PAGE
	PREFACE	vii
I.	AMERICANS ON BOARD	1
II.	AMERICANS DEBATE	12
III.	AMERICANS ASK QUESTIONS	20
IV.	AMERICANS PLAY FOOTBALL	29
V.	AMERICAN FRATERNITIES	38
VI.	AMERICANS AT COLLEGE	46
VII.	AMERICANS HIT THE ROAD	65
VIII.	AMERICANS AT HOME	74
IX.	AMERICAN LAW AND ORDER	89
X.	AMERICANS AND THEIR POLITICS	99
XI.	AMERICANS KEEP ONE GUESSING	112
XII.	AMERICAN PRIVATE ENTERPRISE	125
XIII.	AMERICANS AND "CLASS"	146
XIV.	AMERICAN NEGROES	158
XV.	AMERICANS IN HOLLYWOOD	174
XVI.	AMERICANS AND "YOU BRITISH"	192
XVII.	AMERICANS ARE DIFFERENT	210

TO

MR. AND MRS. FRANK ROBBINS CHAPMAN

ROCHESTER, U.S.A.

PREFACE

MR. KENNETH HARRIS has discovered a new country. Christopher Columbus discovered it, it is true, some time before him, but a good deal has happened there since then. And Mr. Harris, unlike so many other modern travellers, sees the new world with the same sense of wonder as Christopher Columbus. He does not try to be clever about it or laugh at it; he does not look down on it as though he were a superior or more sophisticated person; he frankly wonders and admires, though sometimes critically, sympathises and, I think, understands. Not since Rudyard Kipling published his *From Sea to Sea* has a young Englishman written such an appreciative and rewarding book of travel about the great and vigorous people who to-day constitute the richest and most powerful nation on earth.

For the United States, like the U.S.S.R., is a mighty phenomenon—one which England, the historic balancer of mankind, would do well to try to understand better. It seems curious that, while so many Englishmen in the past thirty years have tried to understand Soviet Russia and to communicate their understanding of her to their countrymen, scarcely anyone, in all the spate of superficial and entertaining travellers' tales on the subject, has really tried to understand and interpret the United States and her people: to penetrate the glittering, artificial exterior of the great Republic and discover the reality, ideal and purpose behind it. Mr. Harris, though without the least pretension to omniscience, has done so. He has done so by faithfully recording—and with an economy and quiet, unassuming gift of selection which seems to me to amount to a kind of genius—the conversations of scores of Americans, mostly young, with whom he talked, not about superficialities, but about the subjects which matter most in the world to Americans and Britons alike. The result is, as I think, an intensely moving and heartening book—one that gives one new hope for the future. I will not delay the reader's pleasure by standing between him and Mr. Harris any longer.

July 1949. ARTHUR BRYANT

CHAPTER I

Americans on Board

SEPTEMBER, 1947. The Oxford Debating Team stood on the quay at Southampton and looked at the *Marine Panther*.

Painted dark brown and yellow, with a faint film of rust on her once white superstructure, the ship looked rather small to be carrying six hundred people across the Atlantic.

"You gentlemen all good sailors?" asked the Customs man.

The others said they were all right. "I don't know," I said. "I've never been on the sea before."

"Well this is the kind of ship to start on," said the Customs man. "Those big ships—well, it's like floating across in an hotel. Now this ship really sails. Last week, in that gale——"

We went aboard. Inside the hull there seemed nothing but bunks, hundreds of them, in the well-decks, round the companion-ways, right up in the stern and crammed into the bows. Our accommodation was on "C" deck. It was a great dark hold, lighted dimly by electric lamps, and reminded me of pictures of the death of Nelson. It was chock-full of bunks arranged in tiers of three. At one end the ship's plates began to converge to form the bows. At the other, a couple of small doors led through the bulkhead into the "Ablutions."

I climbed on to my bunk and watched two yellow-skinned Asiatic-looking members of the crew make up bed after bed with quick, practised fingers. From across the narrow gangway, only a few inches from my head, came a melancholy voice: "You got any seasick stuff?"

I looked across at the speaker. He was dark-haired with a sallow skin. He was taking some powders out of a paper bag. "No," I said. "As a matter of fact, I haven't."

"I sure envy you guys who can take it."

"Take what?"

"The darned sea."

"I don't know that I can, yet."

"Brother, you sure will soon." He shovelled three paperfuls into his mouth and lay down. He put his arms under his head and looked mournfully up at the sunshine.

We took off our suits, and put on the jerseys and slacks which everybody wore for the whole of the voyage. Then we joined the long, thick line which led into the "dining-room." It was a big, low, square chamber with an enormous, brightly shining cooking range in the centre. We filed past the range collecting all our food in one dish, an aluminium tray which had been punched into six little compartments. We carried it to one of the narrow tables and squeezed on to the already jammed benches. The crudeness of the surroundings made a strange contrast with the luxury of the American food. There was no room for shyness in that jostling company. At the end of the meal, a couple of dozen people knew everything about you, and you about them.

I climbed back on to my bunk. "Enjoy that meal?" said the dark-skinned boy.

"Wonderful."

"What part of America you going to?"

"Quite a lot of parts. Forty-three States in five months."

"That's some trip. What you doin'?"

"Debating."

"Debating? Jees! You doing it for a living or sum'p'n?"

"Your Institute of International Education in New York has fixed up a visit by the Oxford Union."

"What's the Union?"

"That's the name of the Oxford Debating Society."

"You doing it all yourself?"

"There's three of us. That fair-haired boy with the pipe over there, that's Anthony Wedgwood Benn. He's the President of the Society. That's Edward Boyle, with the fair hair and the book, coming down the stairs. He's the Librarian."

"Well, I hope you have a good trip," said the dark-haired man. "I'm gonna get some sleep. Jees! When they told me I had to come back on this ship, I nearly stayed European."

"I'm told this ship doesn't roll."

"Sure. That's right. But, boy! How she can pitch. I'll be seeing you when we get to New York."

The next forty-eight hours were miserable. The bunks were suspended by chains which clanked dismally to the rise and fall of the waves. Being a welded ship, the *Panther* never groaned in that human, sympathetic way that most ships have. She plunged along in silence till a big wave struck the bows, and then the whole hull would reverberate like a gong, and we would wake up thinking our last moment had come.

Not until the third day did I manage to stagger up on the deck. I remember how the sun poured in through the open hatch of the boat-deck, as though from another world. On the top step stood a girl with golden hair, blue eyes and a floppy white sweater with the words "Congregational Youth" on the front. There seemed something vaguely evangelical about her.

"You don't look so good," she said.

"I don't feel so good."

"C'mon and sit in the sun." We sat down on a wooden raft. "I wouldn't look at the sea yet," she said.

"I won't."

"I think it'd do you good to come along to the 'Orientations Programme.'"

"To the *what*?"

"'Orientations Programme.' Talks and discussions on Europe for Americans who're on their way back home."

"You should have had them on the way out. It's too late now."

"You miss the point. This boat's full of students and other folks going back home to all parts of the States. When they arrive back in the towns and the villages where they went from, they'll be listened to and believed like experts. It'd be a good thing if we all said roughly the same thing, and sorted out the important impressions from the trivial ones. And it's a good thing for us to get our opinions rubbed down and checked off by discussing them with other people who've been in Europe too."

"Sounds frightfully serious."

"We Americans *are* frightfully serious. When we get worked up about something, we don't go around with forced smiles and stiff upper lips saying, 'Raly, it doesn't mattah.' We make it pretty clear it does matter. We take being serious very seriously." She got briskly to her feet. "C'mon. The opening session starts in five minutes. It'll take your mind off."

"It's not my mind that's bothering me."

"C'mon. You'll never get down that companion-way on your own, anyway."

We descended right into the bowels of the ship to the ship's recreation-room. It was on "D" deck, well lit, flat-floored and stable. About three hundred people sat on chairs, tables or on the floor. Conversation in a dozen languages, American predominating, rose with the throbbing and humming of the engines into an overpowering roar. In the open space in the centre was a microphone connected to the ship's internal radio. At it, in a dark brown, loose-hanging suit, stood a tall, bald, and piercing-eyed man.

"Professor Wiener," said the girl in the white sweater. "Orientator-in-chief. And can he talk." As though obliging with a demonstration, Milton Wiener sent out another mixed blast of sarcasm, persuasion, and exhortation over the ship's radio.

Before he had finished his last ultimatum, the truants came shuffling in, sleepy-eyed, weak-kneed, resentful and cursing, but there. When every seat was filled, Wiener turned his eyes upon the crowd. A glance from him commanded attention—the four Belgian nuns hurriedly put down their beads and the Japanese architects stopped their chattering. After a few seconds pause, he leaped into his full-blooded peptonizing outline of the "Orientations" programme. His voice rose above the noise of waves and engines like Brunhild's above the storm. In ten minutes we were all as orientated as a shipful of lambs. He was irresistibly and inexhaustibly eloquent. Looking back on it now, it is a compliment not a criticism to say that if he had been on the ship much longer, somebody would have pushed him over.

"How d'you feel now?" said the girl in the white sweater as we trooped out with the crowd.

"Better."

"That's the boy. You'll stop being ill when you stop thinking about it."

"H'm."

"Now, as from this afternoon, we're going to divide into groups of a couple of dozen, and discuss things.

Then, in the mornings, we report our findings to the general session, and consolidate."

"I'm going to my bunk this afternoon."

"Quitter."

"These things are meant for you Americans," I said. "I *live* in Europe. I'm orientated already." The girl in the white sweater turned her blue eyes on me. "Well," I said. "Er—whose group am I in?"

"Same as me. 'G' group."

The afternoon found the members of "G" group huddled around the foot of the funnel in raincoats. Some of us were in deck-chairs, and some sat on biscuit-boxes. Now and again the wind blew our hair into our mouths, and sometimes a sheet of spray came over the side. Our group leader was a Quakeress who had been working in Finland. Around her were four or five keen, and well-informed students. There was a French painter, another Frenchman in a yellow pullover who had been in the "Underground," an Italian contessa, a British coalmines manager and his wife, and a lady journalist who wrote for one of those glossy, almost proseless, New York woman's weeklies. There were three middle-aged ladies who were members of a society called "The Associated Countrywomen of the World." Their flying six weeks' visit had rushed them in and out of nearly every European country, but they had taken notes as conscientiously as a Royal Commission.

It was soon discovered that I was the only one with a fountain-pen. I was appointed Group Secretary.

Owing to the variety of points of view, the language difficulty, and the rapidity with which we swung from economic and political to social and cultural topics, there was never a dull moment. The French painter spoke no English, but was passionately argumentative, and we had to keep him informed by making signs, or holding everything up while a Swiss girl translated for him. The other Frenchman in the yellow pullover continually interrupted to say: "We jurst sit here and talk. Why don't we do somethings? My country is starving." Our chief tension-maker was an Australian business man. He was going for the first holiday of his life on a visit to the United States, and travelling by way of India, the Levant, Europe and Great Britain. Anxious to see all he could for once and for all, he had made such huge hops that he had lost his bearings. He was full of the most exciting and highly informative anecdotes, but he could not remember where he had got them. He would announce some staggering fact which would plunge us into silence. "Now let me see," he would say in the electric hush. "Did I see that in Athens, or in Paris?" He would put his head in his hands and groan.

"What have *you* been doing?" I whispered to the girl in the white sweater.

"Czechoslovakia. Church and Welfare work."

"Who pays your expenses?"

"We do of course. Who do you think?" She nudged me. "Sh! We're off again." One of the Associated Countrywomen had said that Europe was in a state of Religious Ferment. "Nonsense," said a girl who had been across with a Roman Catholic mission. "I wish it was," said one of the boys, a Baptist. "Plis, no more talk. Give us foot," said the Frenchman in the yellow pullover. There was a short, sharp wrangle which our group leader drove along under whip and spur to some sort of manageable conclusion.

"That'll do for to-day," she said, mopping her brow. She got up. "We'll leave our good secretary to draw up the minutes."

I almost wished I'd lost my fountain-pen. I looked at the sodden piece of paper. The sea had got on to it once or twice and I had done a lot of rubbing-out. As instructed, I began by writing down the names of the organizations represented in "G" group: "World Student Service," "American Youth Hostels," "Junior Year in Switzerland," "Experiment in International Living," "Rotary," "Friends Committee for European Relief," "Salvation Army——"

"More paper," I said to the girl in the white sweater. "How many voluntary societies have you got in the United States?"

"I don't know. Why?"

"They all seem to be represented in Europe this year."

"They ought to be. The old Isolationist days are over."

"What did we decide about the Religious Ferment? Is it on or off?"

"Off. You being facetious?"

"No, it's just that all this getting together, this discussion and organization, well, it's a bit unfamiliar."

"Don't you think we get things done this way?"

"Well, I'm not feeling seasick any more."

The rains and winds that showered us for the first three days died away, and the sun came out to stay. The time began to go very quickly. By day we pushed on with the Orientations programme, or lay in the sun like flies upon the top deck. By night there was dancing, film shows, and games in the airless recreation room, singing—dance tunes or hymns, depending on whom you were with—and low-pitched conversations on the cool, open decks. The eight Mexican Scouts, always searching for the chance of doing a good deed, showed me photographs of the Eiffel Tower and took me to meet their scoutmaster. A Texan showed me his embroidered leather boots with two-inch heels. "T'hold y'r feet 'n the stirrup."

"We Texans are big fellows," he said to me once.

"But you're quite short."

"Waal, thet's becuz I've lived so lawng in Oklahoma."

I met the man who had been playing a clavichord all over Europe to promote International Understanding. "Now it's America's turn," he explained. I met the man who helped put Captain Webb into the barrel which took him over the Niagara Falls. "A great day for us all," he said with a sigh. A Harvard man from Boston told me about his motor-"caa," and a boy in the next bed told me Brooklyn, New York, was the "world's" best place to live in. The voice I got to like best was that of the Californian boy. "Ah, Cahlifohniah," he used to say, long and soft like a sigh. "Wait till you see Cahlifohniah." His voice brought the caress of the Pacific sea-breeze into that murky hold. One saw the fruits hanging heavy to be plucked, the white surf breaking, the brown limbs lying on the sand.

One night, in mid-ocean, I sat on the deserted top-deck, watching the last red slip of the sun sink into the sea. One of the crew, a plump Spanish-American, was padding round the deck tidying up. As I lay back, lazily computing how much the cigar he was smoking would cost him in Britain, I saw him pick up half a dozen empty Coca-cola bottles and swing them towards the rail. The thought of the waste was galvanizing. "STOP!" I cried, and leaped to salvage them. My foot slipped. We both crashed into a couple of deck-chairs almost invisible under the shadow of a companion-way. There was a female scream of fright followed by male snorts of pain and outrage. I tried to explain my behaviour coolly to the injured parties. The girl stared at me hard.

"Aren't you the Oxford Debater who's been ill?"

"Yes."

Still rubbing themselves, the three held a muttered

consultation. When the young man spoke, his tone was the kind which doctors use to patients who need to be humoured. "Come on, old chap," he said. "I'll help you down to your bunk."

It was strange to see how swiftly we had crossed from a world of want to a world of plenty. Even in the spartan atmosphere of the *Panther* there was new, unheard of, or scarcely remembered, luxury. Ice-cream, luscious, pink and sweet; butter, heaped on the dish in broad, curling dollops; fresh Kadota figs, honey-dew melon, snow-white bread, milk to drink, and two eggs with the thick, sweet, Virginian ham. On the last night of the voyage, we lay in the dusk of a warm October evening off Staten Island. Along the far bank of the Hudson river, we could see the big motor-cars racing along on unrationed petrol. Powerful arcs poured a flood of light down on to highway and across the water. Now and again floated over to us the tuneful notes of their horns and the roar of an accelerating engine. Only to have seen the lights and the stream of motor-cars would have been enough to identify a newer, richer world.

And so at last, rising before the dawn of the ninth day, we gathered on the top- and boat-decks, the six hundred of us, and steamed slowly into the port of New York; straight from Europe into the heart of the New World's greatest city. Through the mists, the Manhattan tracery shone like silver. Beyond it, the Empire State Building and the "up-town" cluster of towers were dark shades pencilled on the blue. The decks were crowded. We were perched on hatches, turrets, the rails, anywhere where we could get a view. The ship looked more like a Thames pleasure launch than an ocean-going steamer. Dutch, French, Italian and British stood wide-eyed with the returning Americans as height after height went by, and more and more of the vast man-made mountains came gently into view. Out on the left was the Statue of Liberty. I had hoped it would gaze down on the ship like the Colossus did at Rhodes, but it was so far away it looked no bigger than a lighthouse. For a moment it held all eyes. To many, coming from lands where liberty had been lost, it symbolized a fresh start and a new hope of freedom. There were sighs, a few half-uttered sounds of joy; and here and there a tear. It was a moment when one was inclined to forget the Dutch stowaway, who had lived on bread and water for a week, and Louis, the ex-Free French journalist, who was booked for Ellis Island. Above us the gulls swooped and curved above the water. The tugs blew cheerful calls upon their hooters, and the *Panther* added hearty blasts to the melodious din. Out on the port side the Statue faded back into the mist. We veered sharply away from it, and slowly glided into our waiting berth.

CHAPTER II

Americans Debate

OUR destination was the Harvard Club. We drove off the quay in a red and yellow cab. Others, green, orange and chequered, raced with us four abreast.

Our driver was black-eyed and swarthy. Above his head was his photograph, set in a certificate which gave his name, address and occupation. He was Fedor Radwitz, born in Warsaw. "You're a Pole," I said.

"No, bud. I'm an American citizen." He flicked the ash from his cigar through the window, and I saw the difference.

We drove up 44th Street and stopped at the club. The street was quiet, but a hundred yards farther along, another crossed it at right angles. Down that one the traffic rushed by in what seemed a solid stream. The colour, the roar, the speed was almost frightening.

"What on earth's that?"

"Fifth Avenue."

The porters came down the steps for our luggage. Our driver pricked up his ears. "You guys is debaters?" he said. "Who you debating against?"

"Sixty American Universities."

"Some junket. Who's foist?"

"Columbia; to-morrow night."

"They've got a hot team. Where next?"

"West Point Military Academy."

"That'll be rugged. Them soldiers sure can talk. Well, have a good trip." He drove off.

We walked round into the next street, to the offices of the Institute of International Education. The Director told us something about American debate. "Not quite the same as it is in Britain," he said. "Some of our Universities have their small, student-run societies, like your Union, but mostly debating is a function of the Department of Speech. It's taught, like history or physics is taught, by people who are trained in it. Not just debate, of course. Speech includes public speaking, discussion, physiology of the voice, and other things too. You can get a degree in it."

"It sounds pretty technical."

"It is—text-books on all aspects of it, conferences of speech teachers, and journals like the *Quarterly Journal of Speech*. By the way, do you ever have 'judged' debates in Britain?"

"Nobody 'judges' apart from the audience."

"Sometimes we have an audience vote here. But usually two or three judges decide. After all, it's such a technical business making a good speech, it needs a man who knows the ropes to judge it."

"If they put trained judges on to us," I said, "we're going to come out very badly."

"Well, I don't know about that," said the Director. "Anyway, I'll look forward to hearing how a typical debate strikes you. Now come out and have a look at Broadway."

He piled us into a taxi, drove us up past the massed batteries of brilliant lamps in Theatreland, and back down Fifth Avenue.

He deposited us, still open-mouthed and blinded, on the steps of the Harvard Club. "Don't forget to drop me a line," he called as he drove off.

Ten days later, his words about American debate came back to me. We had left the big east coast private universities, and were moving across country. That night we were debating at Cherokee State College. At six-thirty, the Professor of Speech led us into the handsome oak-panelled dining-room of the Faculty Club. About thirty people stood waiting for us, teaching staff, students, some prominent local residents and their wives. The president of the university welcomed us. He was forty, looked a fit and athletic thirty, and wore a Balliol tie. He had studied physics and got progged for breaking a window in the Turl.

At dinner I was next to a Dr. Green. Wrinkled, shy, but twinkle-eyed, he was one of the first batch of Rhodes scholars to go over to Oxford. I gathered that Magdalen men had been a bit standoffish. "Expect they hadn't got used to us," he said. Across the table sat a distinguished-looking grey-haired man with a pointed beard. He was Professor Schwab, of the Drama Department, one of America's leading authorities on theatre lighting. Next to him was a tall, dark-eyed brunette of about twenty-three. She had majored in speech, and was now writing her master's treatise on speech correction. Most of that day she had been working in the speech clinic.

Towards the end of the meal she leaned over to us. "Would you gentlemen from Oxford mind if I take my boys out now?" she asked. "They're a bit nervous, and I want to give them a work-out."

We said we would not mind in the least. She got up from the table, and the two American debaters followed her out.

"Big night for her," explained Dr. Green. "Her first international contest."

"Big night for us," I said. "Our first judged debate."

"In that case," he said, "you'd better look at these."

He passed over a sheet of paper headed "Instructions for Judges." Marks were to be awarded under

"Material," "Construction," "Use of Authorities and Quotations," "Delivery" and "Clash." Any of the four speakers who exceeded his ten minutes was to be penalized. After the main speeches, there would be an intermission in which the teams could confer. Each speaker would then have five minutes for "rebuttal." The chief judge was to sum up the debate and deliver the verdict.

"Sounds serious," I said.

"My boy," said Dr. Green, "it is."

"No speeches from the floor?"

"No speeches from the floor."

"The audience might just as well not be there."

"That's right. See, debate over here's to train people how to put a case, not how to sweep a crowd off its feet." He gave a surreptitious look around. "Debate here's so darn dull, they wouldn't get a crowd anyway."

About a quarter to eight, we strolled down the corridor towards the debating hall. On the left I saw a door marked "Speech Office." It was slightly ajar. Through the gap I could see the debate coach sitting holding a stop-watch. In front of her, one of the debaters was prodding the air with an emphatic forefinger. The other was leaning back in a chair, looking at the ceiling and whispering to himself. It was the work-out.

At two minutes to eight we followed our opponents through the packed auditorium up to the stage. I felt we should have been wearing boxing shorts and silk dressing-gowns. On the left of the stage was the Union Jack; on the right were the Stars and Stripes. The teams sat at the desks under their flags. In front of the Americans was a small black-japanned box, the card index of debating points culled by the speech staff.

The Professor of Speech advanced to the rostrum. He spoke into three microphones. The first was the ordinary amplifying system, the second sent it out on the college radio wavelength, and the third was recording the proceedings on a length of magnetized wire, for the files of the Speech Department. "Great occasion," the Professor was saying. "Honour to welcome the British representatives. Different tradition of speech. American team to-night winners of Mid-west inter-state knock-out tournament—good speech makes a safe democracy—brief biographical notes—motion: That basic industries should be nationalized—now calling upon Mr. E. R. Clark of Cherokee to speak first for the affirmative."

E. R. Clark begins. He says a brief but very cordial word of welcome to the British, and gets down to his case. He makes a swift appreciation of the motion, gives a sentence on his general position, and puts forward his four main points. Each is deftly illustrated, supported by a few figures, or a quotation from an expert. His tone is steady, pitched a little above conversational level, rhythmic and persuasive. Now and again he raises a finger, the movement controlled and economical. Occasionally he takes a few slow steps away from the rostrum, sometimes leans on it lightly. His eye flickers regularly to the front row. There sits the time-keeper with eleven cards in his hand. Each is marked with a number from 1 to 10, and the last card bears the legend, "STOP." As 9 appears, the debater begins two sentences of summing up, and adds two or three awkward questions for "the gentlemen from Oxford" to answer. As "STOP" comes up, he closes with a perfect period. He walks quietly to his place. There is no applause. The speech has been a trim set of debating points, excellently prepared, and delivered right to the plexus. Many of the audience know this. But they also know that clapping is not allowed in classrooms, and they are not quite sure whether this is a classroom or a theatre.

The matter, for to-night at least, is soon cleared up.

The Oxford man is at the rostrum. He shocks the audience into life by treating it as though it were there, says what a nice audience it is, and that he doesn't know whether it is more of a pleasure or of an honour to be addressing it. He tells a couple of jokes about Englishmen having no sense of humour, and makes the audience laugh. He says some pleasant things about "my friend who has just spoken," and as a modest smile is creeping on the boy's face, jabs him in the ribs with some unmerited sarcasm. The audience roars: they have smelled blood, and their thumbs are down. The Oxford man spends his few remaining minutes with a quick succession of what he calls "facts," dismisses the questions he has been asked as irrelevant, and throws in a couple of snorters he heard at the last debate. After a stormy peroration, followed by a humble appeal to the wisdom and impartiality of his audience, he flings himself back into his chair, folding his arms and wearing an expression of injured innocence. The audience claps like mad.

After the debate, the chief judge came on the stage. He was sure, he said, that everybody was interested by the difference in style of speaking. It was a close thing, but the verdict went to the British. As he pronounced the "sh" in British, the two American lads ran across the stage. They patted the British warmly on the back and wrung their hands. Then the Professor of Speech shook the British by the hands, and the judges shook hands with the Americans. The British shook hands with the judges. A number of students rushed on to the stage and shook hands with anybody who had a hand free. Everybody was congratulating everybody.

"You're all a credit to the Oxford Speech Department," beamed the wife of the Professor of Speech.

My two colleagues were at the foot of the rostrum where the wire recording of their speeches was already being played back to them. "I'm afraid we aren't lucky enough to have a Speech Department over there," I said.

"You haven't? Then what do you have?"

"Well, there's nothing like that in the curriculum. If you want to debate, you join a club or something."

"You do? Well, for goodness' sakes. D'ye hear that, Elmer? These boys got it all up themselves. Well, for goodness' sakes!"

"You boys used *humour*," said the Professor of Speech's daughter, in the tone of a housemaster's wife who has caught a prefect smoking.

"Wonderful audience appeal," the Professor of Speech kept saying. He bustled over to us. "Wonderful audience appeal. I shan't rest till my boys have got that too."

"Here, Elmer," said his wife. She whispered briefly in his ear.

"Huh?" he said. He moved off quickly.

A tall, slinky blonde glided into the group. I had seen her sitting in the front row, looking very interested. It appeared, however, that she was writing a treatise on accents. "Your London accents," she said, "or do you call it the King's accent? Boy, oh boy! I hardly heard a word you said. I just sat there, rigid, listening to that accent!"

Up came the debate coach. Her eyes were agreeably wide. "You boys were dynamite," she said. "Is this true what I hear, about you teaching yourselves?"

"Well, more or less."

"Don't you even have a coach around?"

"No," I said. "I'm beginning to see what we're missing."

As we walked out I bumped into the president and Dr. Green. "Enjoy yourself?" said the president.

"Wonderful," I said.

At that moment the tall blonde shimmered up again. She was making notes in a big note-book. "Do you know, Mr. President," she said, "they don't have phonetics in the curriculum at Oxford?"

"Well, well, well," said the president. As he pushed me into his big black Buick he gave me a broad wink. "Well, well, well," he said again.

CHAPTER III

Americans Ask Questions

ONE American in seventy is at the university: two million out of a hundred and forty millions. The black-japanned box of the Speech Department talks for thousands at a time.

One of the thirty debates on Nationalization is coming to an end. The chairman announces that, after the verdict, there will be an Open Forum. Questions may be addressed to any speaker.

They come thick and fast. From the back of the auditorium comes a loud, harsh, foreign-sounding voice: "Ze British government have taken special powers which have never been known in peace-time. Zey can direct industry and capital as zey like. How is this different from Nazi Germany, please?"

There is a rumble of assent. The speaker is a member of the medical staff. Everybody knows he was driven from Heidelberg in 1936.

One of the British speakers walks to the microphone. He has learned that a bold, country-proud answer is better than the right answer, even if he knew it. ". . . and if the British people don't like it, they can sack this government at the next election. Elections in Britain are free." There is a general murmur of satisfaction.

A smoothly-dressed, bow-tied, elegant young man rises to his feet. His voice is soft and cultured, though his dark hair is cropped almost to the scalp. "Can the gentlemen from Oxford assure us that elections in England might not go the same way as free elections did in Germany?" Another rumble. ". . . Elections go that way," says the Oxford man, "only when the democratic spirit dies in the hearts of the people. Do the last ten years suggest that that is happening to the British?" Applause. The young man smiles in a friendly way, nods, and sits down.

Up springs a flaxen-haired nymph with a scarlet ribbon round her head. In one hand is a big note-book, in the other a copy of Professor Hayek's *Road to Serfdom.* She is far too pretty to be asking awkward questions. "If the miner cannot leave the pit, is he living in a free country?" Loud applause. "The miners voted for this government," says the Oxford man. "I'm sure the audience know that line of Wordsworth: 'the prison unto which we do condemn ourselves no prison is . . .'!" There is a dubious muttering, some ragged applause. Wordsworth hasn't made it. The girl, looking prettier and more determined than before, is on her feet again. "Then why do the miners strike?" she cries breathlessly. There is a long, deep growl of approval. "Because they want to show the world they're as free as America's miners."

Up in the gallery, there is a rustle. All heads swivel round. A big, broad-shouldered youth is on his feet, patiently waiting for the noise to die down. He was pointed out to the Oxford men earlier in the day as a B.M.O.C.—Big Man on Campus. He wears a bright canary-coloured pullover, and the short, fur-collared jacket he wore when he bombed Berlin. "The gen'l'men from England," he says, in a slow, thoughtful tone, "tell us that the British people are going through a crisis—a kind of economic Dunkirk. Well, why don't they send for Winston Churchill?" There is loud and prolonged applause. The man from Oxford walks slowly to the microphone. He leans across the rostrum in a confidential manner. The silence is tense. "As a matter of fact," he says, "I really don't know." There is a deafening roar. The audience is with him to a man. If there is one thing they will lift the roof off for, it is a plumb confession of ignorance.

In nearly every audience there would be one or two of the less conservative thinkers whom the Americans call "liberals" or "radicals." At San Francisco and Los Angeles, the barrage from the Right was almost exceeded by the onslaught from the Left. "Nationalization kills initiative. Why doesn't your government free industry instead of suffocating it?" followed immediately by: "Why doesn't your government raise a capital levy to check inflation and bring in equality?" There would be twenty or thirty people on their feet at once, each trying to deliver a question. "One at a time, please," the chairman would say. "Why don't your Socialists get out and let your business men get in?" And just as often: "Why don't your Labourites quit, and let some real Socialists plan the economy?"

Often it was suggested that the plight of Europe, and Britain in particular, was due to forsaking the principles of Private Enterprise. A return to them was advocated persistently as the key to recovery. One American debater was asked if he thought the United States had the answer to Europe's difficulties. "Yes," he cried with confidence. "If Europe will do what we say, she will be on her feet within a year or two. Let her provide incentives, remove unequal taxation, free exports from government red tape, and learn salesmanship from the United States."

Another offered Europe the "Four I's. Industry, Initiative, Intellect and Imagination." To this an Oxford man suggested that Britain had suffered great damage to her economy because of the blasting her people and her property had taken in the war to defend democracy. The audience applauded warmly. He said that much had been said of the American Free Enterprise which had won the war, but he had heard that not a wheel had turned, nor a whistle blown till the government had announced its bonus and royalty scales. This remark was greeted with a delighted roar, in which the beaming faces of two Republican Congressmen were very noticeable. The Americans rather enjoy hard, straight hitting; they hate innuendo.

After the Open Forum, there might be an informal reception for speakers, members of the faculty, guests and students. The latter seemed to have a very black-and-white way of thinking about freedom and control. "Look here now," we would often have to say, "it isn't fair to say that Nationalization and Direction of Labour go together."

"Well, they're together in Britain."

"Yes, but they're not the *same*. You've had nationalization of a sort with your Tennessee Valley Scheme, but nobody directed your labour."

"Well, why do you direct yours?"

"For the same reason it was directed in war-time. Every bit of it counts; it's being directed because we're in a hole, not because we're Reds."

"Oh! Ah!"

"As for monopolies, you don't like them any more in the States than we do. You've got your famous Trust-busting act."

"Sure . . . I see what you mean . . . but tell me, how *can* you be free if you're told where to work?"

A big, burly man comes up, balancing a cup of coffee in one hand, and a sandwich in the other. His manner is bluff, but his smile is friendly. "We've had a taste of what your government's trying to do," he says. "Called it the New Deal. We paid good dollars for men to dig up the road and fill it in again. That's planning for you."

"That's *bad* planning. What about TVA, the schools and the new streets?"

"Sure. But those things didn't cure the depression. In 1929 we got into a slump. Things were mighty tough. I got cleaned out myself. But all we could do was to wait till it was over and start over again. We're tough enough to do that over here."

"But surely you don't think it's a bad thing to lessen a depression, or to avoid one, if there are ways of doing so?"

"No, I don't. But not at the price of losing the only things which make life worth living, and which make this country what it is. If you don't believe in Private Enterprise, you don't believe in America. This country was born that way, and it'll go on living and fighting that way."

Into the group comes a boy who says he is reading economics. After one or two unfortunate excursions into economic theory, he explains that by economics he really means business administration. "You ask us to lower tariffs," he says, "and you keep our goods out artificially. How come?" We discuss Britain's trading position in relation to the United States. "Then I don't see what you've got to complain about," he says. "You were on top in the nineteenth century; now Uncle Sam's on the ball."

"But the positions *aren't* the same. In the nineteenth century, the richer we British became, the more we spent —we bought over half our food and most of our raw materials. The United States can feed herself, and she needs hardly anything from outside."

"That's a point. You British sure know some of the answers."

"We're learning them fast—through the skin."

"Say, how hard *are* things over there? Getting pretty tough, I guess." The voice, now that we have left figures and got to human beings, is sympathetic, almost gentle. I give him a pamphlet on Britain's food crisis. He stares at the cover. "What's this—England and Wales only as big as all Oregon?"

"A little smaller."

He goes off with an incredulous whistle, turns on his heel and comes back. "Say, I hate to bother you fellers, but my folks run a store back home. If you can give me a few addresses, they'd get a great kick out of sending a parcel or two across." Three or four bystanders also start pulling out their pens. They have not heard of Keynes, but they have kind hearts.

One of the debaters comes up with a young lady and gentleman. It is Mrs. Virgil P. Smith, née Griffiths, a war-bride from South Wales. She introduces me to her husband who is studying agriculture. "I guess you'll have to let Canada go," he says.

"*Let it go?*"

"Why yes. Too expensive to keep up."

"Mrs. Smith; what have you been telling your husband about Canada?"

"Nothing. Indeed now."

We have a little talk about the position of the various constituent members of the Commonwealth. "So you see, Mr. Smith, Nationalization can't 'spread,' as you put it, like the measles to, say, New Zealand; and Canada could say good-bye to us to-morrow if she wished to."

"I see. Thanks very much." They all *see* very quickly, but they don't seem to *think* as much as they could. They like things in tabloid form, not spun out in thin, self-generating chains of reason. They like truths served up as they are in the laboratory and the workshop, in solid, palpable, authenticated handfuls. They are not used to feeling for it with their fingertips in the dark places where political theory and practice meet. But what they know, they know. It goes right in with the blood.

"Why don't you Oxford guys speak English? What's 'æsthetic' mean?"

There was no sign of Isolationism in debate, discussion or conversation—with one exception. He was a teacher in a south-western state university. About forty years of age, he was serious, careful, learned and respected. "The question is," he said, "is Western Europe capable of re-civilizing itself, or is it finished? If it can't be resurrected, and if we over here were sure that it couldn't, it would be our duty not to waste time and money on it, but to try and prevent this new, untried world from going the same way."

The swiftness with which American opinion has advanced from Isolationism to Internationalism struck us in the questions we were asked on "World Federal Government." The existence in every college of "World Federalist" societies, and the selection of "World Federal Government" as the motion for the 1948 All-American Debating Tournament, meant that our questioners, if starry-eyed, were well-informed. "What do you think about World Federal Government in Britain?" they said.

"Well, to be quite frank, I don't believe we *do* think about it much."

"Some folks say you British don't want it—that you're too smart to work for a conference where you'd have to start off square with everybody, that you're scared in case you lose the empire, and your power in Europe."

"Really? What else do they say?"

"Some say you're just too unimaginative to try the scheme; others say you're too cynical."

"I hope somebody points out, also, that we're rather busy supporting UNO, which seems the only really practicable road to world peace, and that your government, by the way, is doing the same."

"Sure, surc. I was only kidding. Say, have you heard Cord Meyer, the World Federalist big-shot, speak?"

"Yes, I have."

"What d'you think of him?"

"He's a fine man. His analysis of the world's problems is brilliant. But I'd like him to say more about how World Government is going to be set up, and how it's going to work when it *is* set up; you know—the practical side of it all."

From older Americans we sometimes heard criticism of the World Federalists. They were "too idealistic, too ineffective." It seemed to us, however, that they had achieved the very practical result of interesting in Europe, thousands of Americans who otherwise might not have thought about it much. As Europeans we felt very grateful to them.

The most often-asked single questions were about Russia. Did the British fear and distrust the Russians as much as the Americans did? Were the British people as fearful of war as the Americans?

But it was not America's fear of Russia, great as it was, which stood out as our chief impression of American thinking: it was their passionate faith in Private Enterprise. Sometimes it was spoken of with an almost religious degree of feeling, dogmatic, glad, reverent. Against the imagined background of world Communism it shone like a crusader's sword—yet, a weapon for defence, of home and health and historical values. No less did it shine out and lighten the domestic scene. Labour, Capital and Government seemed the sacred instruments by which prosperity and content came with almost mechanical precision. American youth seemed not ill-pleased with the inheritance for which it had recently been to war. It was ready, if necessary, to fight again.

CHAPTER IV

Americans play Football

FOOTBALL runs in American veins like a second blood. A banker will break off a conference to hear the Harvard-Yale game, the Stock Exchange shuts early when Army is playing Navy.

The big games are played by the universities. The amateur sides of Michigan and Notre-Dame occupy the places held in Britain by Arsenal and Aston Villa. Football is the greatest single centre of interest on the campus. The stadium, holding twenty, thirty, anything up to eighty thousand people, dwarfs the whole of the academic buildings put together. When big games approach, the boys wear coloured buttons on their lapels—"Beat Yale," "Beat Williams," "Beat Chi," or whoever is the enemy. Girls do for a quarter-back what they would not do for a poet. The wives, the mothers, of faculty members go to the game and discuss it afterwards. Thousands flock in for the game from the outlying countryside; students are outnumbered by residents, out-of-town dwellers, and university "alumni." Every Saturday brings a crop of Wembleys.

The game we saw was small and comparatively quiet. Abernethy College were playing Dale City. We got to the ground forty minutes before the kick-off. Nearly every seat was full. Our stand ran the whole length of the field. Another, lower and uncovered, ran along the opposite side. Both ends were open, but a few people stood just behind the tall, Rugby-looking posts. The field, very green in the sunlight, was divided by white lines which ran every ten yards, parallel to the goal-lines. Judging by the conversation, everybody on our side was for Abernethy. Dale City supporters were pouring out of motor-coaches and taking up their positions in the stands across the way. Below us, right on the front rows and upon the half-way line, was the Abernethy College orchestra. Clad in white flannels and blue-peaked caps, they played stirring martial airs. Leading them was the Professor of Music. He wore a fawn lounge suit, but he, too, wore a blue cricket cap. A hundred yards away, with his back to him, the Dale City Music Professor was raising his baton for the Dale City band to start to play. At each corner of the field were large radio amplifiers. One began to boom just above us. Through it, giving the names and weights of the players, came the voice of the Professor of Speech.

Twenty minutes before the kick-off, the teams ran on to the field. Abernethy wore maroon, and Dale City blue. All their breeches were yellow. Their helmets shone like gold in the sun; their padded knees and stiff shoulders gave them the appearance of armoured gladiators. There were sixty-six of them, eleven a side and twenty-two spares. "ABERNETHY," roared our side of the field. "DALE CITY," roared the crowd on the other side. "BIM! BANG! BIM!" went the two orchestras.

From out of the front of the stand streamed twelve white-clad, well-formed figures. Six were sparkling-eyed girls with thick, abandoned hair; six were nimble, slim-hipped boys. For a moment they conferred with a thirteenth figure who wore a tall red hat. Then they scattered down the touch-line, boy, girl, boy, girl, a figure posted every ten or fifteen yards. The boy with the red hat shot up his hand. "A!" cried the twelve voices as one. "A!" bawled the crowd. "B!"—"B!" "E!"—"E!" and so on through the name, then: "ABERNETHY! RAAAAAAH!" roared the crowd, and "YEAH!" cried the cheer-leaders, and over and over in a consummate somersault went the boy in the red hat, as the twelve ran back to the front of the stand, and "CRASH! BANG! CRASH!" went the Abernethy band. Dale City were working on similar lines.

The referee arrived. He wore white plus-four flannel trousers with black stockings, a black and white striped shirt, a red bow-tie and a flat, white flannel cap. This dress was to distinguish him from the players. With him he brought an assistant referee, two touch-judges, two men with an apparatus for measuring distances up to ten yards, a football, a whistle and a revolver. They held a conference in the middle of the pitch—it was the only part in which there was any room left. The Abernethy first team was practising sprint starts, and the reserves were doing P.T. exercises; the remaining eleven were loping lugubriously round the perimeter. Dale City firsts were throwing the ball hard at one another, and their seconds were lying on their backs kicking their legs in the air. The other eleven had split into two sets of five, who were trying to push each other back, shoulder against shoulder. The odd man out was walking on his hands. Suddenly the referee's consultations broke up. Touch-judges and men with measuring rods took up their posts, and the surplus forty-four players hurried from the field. They sat on long benches on their respective touch-lines, with blankets on their backs, and helmets neatly laid out in rows. The teams lined up facing one another in crouching postures, the crowd's roar swelled to a chant under the second attempt of the cheer-leaders, the bands blew for all they were worth, the referee fired his gun, and the great ball-game was on.

Everything seemed to happen out of what was called the "down." When it was "their down," the team arranged itself in a roughly triangular formation. The forwards, when the whistle was blown, would pass back the ball among the quarters, who would pass or run according to the "play" which had been prescribed by the captain. The other team would just block, and try to prevent them from making enough "yardage" to qualify for another "down." If ten yards weren't made in four downs, the ball went to the other team, who then tried out their "plays."

Abernethy were being driven back. Out streamed the cheer-leaders. "FIGHT, BOYS, FIGHT!" thundered the crowd rhythmically. "ABERNETHY! RAAAAAH!" "YEAH!" shrilled the fuglers. Abernethy were forced back nearer their goal-line. Out came the cheer-leaders. "HOLD THAT LINE!" they commanded. "HOLD THAT LINE!" bellowed the crowd. Over the other side, the Dale City cheer-leaders were executing gloating dances, and pretty, mincing, coquettish movements with shoulders and wrists. "NICE GOING DALE CITY!" roared their fans. Out of the shambles at the foot of the goal-posts, which were quivering like aspens as body after body slammed into them, a flying figure emerged hugging the ball. The Abernethian made a gallant thirty yards and crashed into two beefy Dale City "Interference" men. There was an audible thud as two heads met. The third had butted the Abernethian irresistibly in the stomach. "Whoooh!" roared the crowd, this time unled. The Abernethian was carried groaning to the touch-line. "Good game, Heinz!" shouted the leaders. "GOOD GAME, HEINZ!" bawled the crowd. "That guy's soft," said a man behind me.

Everybody, including the players, kept half an eye on

the coaches. They were positioned on their touch-lines, within speaking distance of the reserves. From time to time, a word from the coach would send one of these diving for his helmet and sprinting out at top speed to the scrum. The returning man would trot in, and, before he sat down, make his report to the coach. The Abernethy coach preserved an Olympian calm. Even when the college team seemed about to crumble on the back line, he sat immovable and inscrutable on an upturned bucket. The Dale City coach, on the other hand, was more demonstrative. He danced and cursed on the touch-line like an eccentric cheer-leader. When things went badly, he clutched his forehead with his hand.

Half-time came, and no score. Over the radio, the hoarse voice of the Professor of Speech—he had followed the game with a running commentary—gave place to the tones of the debate coach. He read out the half-time scores of neighbouring matches. Cheers, groans or stony silence greeted each item. "Don't forget the dance to-night," concluded the debate coach. "Come and get hep in the Union Dance Hall; only half-a-dollar. Tuxedo or business suit."

Now the Abernethy band was forming ranks in front of the stand. Led by a beautiful girl in knee-high, red kid-leather boots and a short, swirling skirt, they began to march to a military rhythm round the touch-lines. As they passed the opposite stand, they were joined by two boys carrying the Stars and Stripes. The Dale City band stood at attention as the girl drum-major led the Abernethians down the half-way line, back towards the Abernethian stand. She twirled her staff with an expert flourish; sometimes she threw it in the air and caught it. About ten yards from the line, the band halted. Marching with a kind of cross between the military slow-step and a goose-step, the colour party carried the flag out on its own in the front. The band played the national anthem, and we all sang it. Then they executed a series of impressive military manœuvres, and withdrew. This was followed by a briefer demonstration, and on a smaller scale, by the Dale City band.

The game began again. Abernethy, it was clear, were making a desperate stand. Band, cheer-leaders and team were making a concerted effort. "FIGHT!" roared the fans. "SMACK!" went the helmets. "BIM! BAM! BIM!" went the band. Round and round spun the exciting skirts of the golden-haired girls, up and over went the tumbling boys. Dale City were breaking. A steady flow of players came and went from the benchful of reserves. "Jump on them," yelled a matron sitting on my left. "Play fair, Ref.," shouted her husband, adding as an afterthought: "You rotten bum!" One sensed that the great moment was coming. Abernethy had forced their crab-like way up to a point thirty yards from the Dale City goal. The ball went into the scrum. Back it came and the quarters started running. Each one was crashed into by a Dale City man—but one man got away. With great speed and dexterity he ran up-field, and collected a perfectly lobbed pass. Sconcing it under his arm he ran for the goal. Everybody leaped to their feet. He dodged his tackle. Everybody stood on their seats. There was a blurred glimpse of him hurling himself over the line, and the universe was one long sobbing shout of joy, a mass of clapping hands and waving hats. "ABERNETHY!" cried the leaders. "ABERNETHY!" croaked the Professor of Speech on the radio. "RAAAH!" roared the crowd. A deathly hush hung over the Dale City stands. Their coach stood for a moment in silence. Then, with one dramatic gesture, he purged the team throughout.

Maurois says that the English treat war as sport. The Americans seem to treat sport as war.

I turned round to Lew who was sitting on my left. It was he who had brought me to the match. "Lew, what happens if a chap goes out and doesn't do what the coach tells him?"

"Gosh!" Lew was so shaken, he stopped cheering. "He'd be hunked right back."

"Well, apart from the exercise, then, this is a game for coaches."

"Say, what d'you mean? The coach knows all the 'plays.' Who'd work out the plays and change the team over if he weren't there?"

"But that's what I mean. It's like a game of chess, with animated chessmen. Where's the fun for the players?"

"But where'd be the fun for us if it was all left to them?"

An article I read later revealed that steps were being considered to relax the grip which the coaches had on the game. In first-class football, it seemed, they were connected by telephone to scouts armed with telescopes sitting along the roofs of the stands. Their salaries were enormous. A good coach was paid more than any ten professors on the campus put together. What the president of Harvard was paid was pin-money beside what was paid to the Harvard football coach. On some campuses, the appointment of a new one, or the dismissal of the old, brought violent headlines in the students' newspapers, and full reports in the leading state journals. There would be a crisis of almost political aspect.

"How do you know the words of the cheers. Lew?"

"Pep meetings. Cheer rallies."

"What are they?"

"'Bout once a week the coach and the teams come out

in front of the fans. The coach says a word to the fans. Then the cheer-leaders get to work on 'em. Get 'em worked up ready."

"Ready for what?"

"Ready for Saturday. Say, if you wanna be able to cheer, Ken, you got to be in pretty good training."

"Does anybody ever get badly hurt, Lew?"

"Sometimes. Not often. Not as often as in that Soccer game of yours. No pads! Whew!"

The game ended with victory for Abernethy. Haggard, damp-eyed, as exhausted as the players—far more weary-looking than the reserves—the crowds poured out and home.

"Well, what d'you think of it, son?" I looked round. The speaker was the librarian.

"Well, between you and me, sir, I didn't care for it very much."

"Huh-huh! You know we're having a new stadium next season."

"So I hear. Everybody seems pretty pleased about that."

"Sure. Sure they are. Now, if they had one less dressing-room than they're planning for, I could have my new wing for the library, and old Jenkins could have his extension for the music-room. Do you know, son, millions of pounds pour in and out of the university every year on account of this football. When Chicago chucked university football a few years ago—they used the stadium for atomic research—there was nearly a riot. I hope it's not the same in Britain."

I thought I had better not try to answer that one. "Well, money or no money, sir, padding or no padding, it's a pretty tough game, American football."

"That's true. A man needn't be ashamed of being able to play it. H'm! No padding, you say in English football? Be a good thing, perhaps, if there weren't any padding here."

"Good Lord, sir! The game couldn't possibly be played without padding!"

"Yes. Well, that would be too bad, wouldn't it? Well, have a good trip, young man. Have a good trip."

CHAPTER V

American Fraternities

"WE hate being lonesome." For all the ice-boxes and the electric washers, the country is vast, the mountain barriers high, the forest still impassable. Always there the old danger of being cut off.

The peculiar problem of being lonely in a crowd is tackled for the student by the Fraternity. The Fraternity is a nation-wide association, with chapters in each college or university. The name of each is usually made up of two or three Greek letters. Membership is by invitation. Each Fraternity tries to elect the eligible freshmen; freshmen vie with each other for admission to the most select houses. Some Americans say that the societies are exclusive, snobbish, typed. Others say that they create intimate, internal loyalties without which the young stranger from "the sticks" would be lost among the other ten thousand. Most students get elected. The others miss many social and physical comforts, and go through the university knowing that nobody wanted them.

The battered old Ford chugged steadily down the street. On either side were grass verges, cherry trees in bloom, and behind tiny box hedges large, comfortable-looking detached houses.

"Alpha Omega on the left," said Sam Wertheimer, at the wheel. "Beta Kappa on the right; Kappa Kappa Delta next door, and here we are: the best of the lot, Omega Phi." We pulled up with an explosive snort outside a big, red-roofed house made of white timber. On the grass, near the front door, two or three boys were lying sprawled in the sun.

Sam was trying to turn the engine off. "Shan't borrow this one again," he said.

"I thought this was your car."

"No *sir*. Belongs to one of the pledgers."

"One of what?"

"Pledgers. If a guy wants to join a Fraternity, first he has to be invited. If he's invited, he's got to do a spell of—well, probation. Do the odd jobs, tidy up, make himself useful, answer the phone."

"Like fagging."

"Like what?"

I explained. "Well," said Sam, "seems a mighty big difference to me. I guess your kids don't compete to become fags."

He led the way into the hall. There were thirty or so boys lounging around on sofas, talking and laughing in little groups. They wore check or fawn trousers, bright jerseys and pullovers, red, yellow or Fair Isles pattern, and "loafers." Two boys wore bright red flannel shirts, outside, not inside, the belt. Some of them carried thigh-length warms. All had their hair cut short; some had it cropped so that it bristled.

Down the stairs ran a tall, handsome youth carrying a football helmet. "This is the president of the House," said Sam. "Ken, I'd like for you to meet Bill Macdonald."

"Hi-ya, Kenny," said the president. "Glad to see you. You debaters are working to a rugged schedule. How you making out?"

"O.K."

"Fine. You don't let it get you down. Does everywhere you go ask what y' think of the States?"

"Yes."

"Waal, what *do* you?"

"It's wonderful."

There was a roar of laughter. Now other boys had crowded around. They wasted no time waiting to be introduced. "I'm Tom Bates. Glad to meet yuh." "Hullo, Ken; glad y' dropped in. I'm Ike Jones." "H'lo, Kenny. Hope you have a swell time here."

"Say, Ken," said the president. He put a friendly arm round my shoulder. "I'd sure like to have you meet our House-mother."

"House who?"

"Why, our House-mother, Kenny. Don't you know who she is? Nearly every Frat House has one." We walked down the hall to the House-mother's tiny suite. Her sitting-room was a pretty little nest of pink and blue. On the floor was a large sewing-basket and a pair of socks. A big fellow with ginger hair was sitting on a small chair twiddling his bare toes. "Mrs. Smith," said the president. "I'd like you to meet our friend Ken. He's going to eat here."

"We're here just to add a touch of home," said Mrs. Smith. Her kind eyes and silvery hair seemed to be doing it. "You know, our boys look pretty big and tough; but a lot of them miss their homes. Do English boys love their mothers, Mr. Harris?"

"Er—yes, I should say so, Mrs. Smith."

"American boys certainly love theirs. Sometimes too much."

We went back into the hall. A lad wearing a white tunic over his dominoed shirt came up to the president. "Chow's up, Bill," he said. The president crossed to the House-mother's door. As she came in, he gave her his arm gravely. Everybody rose, and stood in silence as the pair walked slowly to the head of the table. The president sat her down, and took his stand at the other end. We followed to the table. He said a brief grace, and we began to eat. More lads in white jackets—they were the duty squad for that week—replaced the dishes of stew with ice-cream and fruit. There were big jugs of milk, and tumblers of water.

After the meal we all went into the sitting-room. The boys came round and asked questions about the debating tour, Oxford, and the food situation in Britain. "Now, just how Red is Mr. Attlee? Would he be willing to face up to Stawlin?" Again, no waiting to be introduced. With an open, unself-conscious, natural poise, they came up smiling, and holding out their hands. If the president, or Sam, became involved in some other conversation, and for a moment the guest seemed to stand alone, one or two boys would move forward and keep the conversation going. I wondered what might happen to an American visitor in an Oxford common-room.

When the group broke up, I was shown round the house. Upstairs was a games-room, a small reading-room, and a couple of guest-rooms. The walls were panelled in some rich dark wood, and the heavy hangings were in red. The few studies were plainly furnished and small. There were two large dormitories, each holding a dozen or so double-bunked wooden beds. Their appearance was spartan.

"Not many of you get much privacy."

"What do you want that for, Kenny?"

"Working?"

"We've got classrooms."

"Reading?"

"There's the library."

"Having a young lady in to tea."

"Take her out in the auto."

Downstairs at the door, Mrs. Smith was waiting to say good-bye. "Don't let the boys drag you about," she said. "They don't understand that talking's tiring. If they do that, you come back to my room and have a good nap."

This time Sam had borrowed a shiny, streamlined Packard. "This must be one of the better Fraternity Houses," I said, as he pressed the starter. "And I liked the House-mother."

"*Our* House-mother, Kenny," said Sam.

There is a good deal of singing at Fraternity Houses. Singing at meals, when guests are present, is a traditional kind of compliment. The first chorus might start quite suddenly, perhaps half-way through the soup. There seemed to be an unwritten law that everybody had to join in and sing his share; your neighbour might suddenly break off his chain of statistics for the Minnesota wheat crop, and start some rollicking song of the sea. When the song had finished, conversation would be resumed; then, as it got under way, another tune would break out—this time a love ballad. Swallowing his potato hastily, your neighbour would begin to croon soulfully. On the whole, the music was spirited and well sung, except for some over-sweet cadences, and patches of sentimental vamping. The words were interesting.

The Cannon Song

In Cambridge town we have a team
  That knows the way to play,
With Cambridge spirit back of them
  They're sure to win the day.
With songs and cheers we'll rally round
  The cannon as of yore,
And Cambridge halls shall echo
  With the Cambridge Tigers' roar.

Crash through that line of blue
And send the backs on round the end,
Fight! Fight! For every yard.
Cambridge's honour to defend, Rah! Rah! Rah!
Roar, Tiger, siss-boom-bah,
And we'll fight with a vim that is dead sure to win
For old Cambridge.

"Can't You Climb Up?"

The first year that Balliol did enter the league
She paralysed Magdalen and Queen's,
The first year that Balliol did enter the league
She paralysed Magdalen and Queen's.
Can she play ball! Can she play ball!
Can she play ball with Magdalen and Queen's
Can she play ball! Can she play ball!
Can she play ball with Magdalen and Queen's.

I have changed the American proper names into some British titles which would correspond. Imagine the students in an Oxford college hall doing the singing, the Senior Tutor, the Warden, and perhaps the Head of some other college, tapping the table and putting in their siss-boom-bah, and you have a fair idea of a Fraternity guest-night.

Sometimes, even after lunch, the members of the chapter will sing one of their own Fraternity songs. Again, the music is pleasant, but the serious, almost soulful manner in which the syncopated tune is sung is not easy to get used to.

Three Times Three

(last verse)
Then pledge the toast "Our Chapters," boys, their glory and renown,
And fill the glasses up, and drink the liquor down;

And only stop for breath, boys, to formulate the cry,
"Here's three times three, long life to thee, our glorious Delta Phi!"

(chorus)
Here's three times three, long life to thee, our glorious Delta Phi!
Here's three times three, long life to thee, our glorious Delta Phi!
We're the jolliest of societies, and no one can deny,
We're the verriest, merriest chapters of the glorious Delta Phi.

American boys are much less shy about singing, and far better at it, than British. In many places there were singing nights once or twice a week, and the number of small glee clubs and amateur octets was striking. On the other hand, instrumental music, and the collecting of gramophone records, seemed to be less popular than over here.

Once or twice I was invited to have a meal with the female kind of Fraternity. The Sorority Houses which I saw were very comfortably, almost richly, furnished. Before the meal I was taken into the drawing-room. Here I met the House-mother—there are no House-fathers—and was introduced to the girls. Like the boys they came up with the same easy smile, the outstretched hand and the same open charm—"Why, hullo, Mr. Harris." Then they perched on the arms of chairs, or sat round the floor on the grey or pale blue carpets like a scattering of spring crocuses. Every time I said something, they laughed the short, tinkling laugh which the Japanese girls have in *The Mikado.*

I enjoyed all my visits to the Sororities until the time came to rise after lunch. Then, as each girl stood with bowed head behind her chair, we sang a song about the Fraternity Girl, the Sigma Kappa Girl, or the Alpha Phi Girl, depending on which Sorority we were in. The verses said that she was beautiful, golden-haired, blue-eyed and sweet-natured. They all loved her and wanted to be like her. When they came to the very sentimental end of the ditty, they sang it again. This time they "swung" it. The contrast between the frank, sensible, grown-up, healthy charm of these girls and the half-baked, adolescent fantasy of their song was something I could never understand.

Some of the Fraternities are guilds rather than chapters of an association. The debaters have a nation-wide Fraternity, for instance, and there is a very select academic Fraternity which has only a few hundred members in it throughout all forty-eight states. Once elected, the student never resigns. He is Alpha Omega, Delta Phi for life. He wants it that way, and that is how it is.

"What happens to those who don't get elected to a Fraternity, Sam?"

"That's just too bad for them, Kenny. They get through, though."

CHAPTER VI

Americans at College

OUT of the Pullman car window, the prairie stretches away back to the horizon—land, land, land, brown and yellow, rising and falling gently, limitless like the sea. Not even a wire fence borders the track; the line is at ground-level, and the metals look like cotton strips, neither strong nor deep enough to stay in place. Through many a fair-sized mid-west town the train has passed plumb, with only traffic-lights to warn the motor-cars and the walkers that they must not cross the un-gated road. Through Ohio villages and Missouri townships, the west-bound express thunders across the High Street at all hours of the day and night, whistle moaning like a banshee, bell clanging, and the huge headlamp sending a broad beam two hundred yards ahead.

Walking down the corridor, past the ice-water fountain and the bright reproductions of Cézanne and Matisse, we come to the diner. Only the head waiter is a white man; he wears a dark suit, with a grey-striped waistcoat. From the breast-pocket sticks out a clump of pencils. He gives one to each passenger so that he can write out his own order.

"I'd like another whisky."

"Sorry, sir. No drinks."

"But, dash it; I had one only five minutes ago."

"Yes, sir. But since then we've crossed a state border. This state's dry."

As we finish lunch, the whistle begins to blow short

jerky blasts. The bell is clanging. Scattered homesteads are appearing, one or two big sheds, a road—like a thin strip of sticking-plaster on the brown face of the prairie. Now there is a warehouse, a lofty building with the name of a big cereal firm on it. The train is slowing down to a halt. This is our next stop: Rocky City.

When we get out, we find that there is no station. We have alighted right in the middle of the street. The booking office is between a barber's shop and a garage. Cars drive up and down on either side of the track.

"Pardon me. Are you the three gentlemen from Oxford?"

"We are."

"That's fine. I'm Jack Erlinger from the Speech Department, and this is Bob East from the Union reception committee who'll look after you while you're with us. What about your bags?"

"I'm afraid there's an awful lot of them. Nine."

"That's O.K.—we've got a car. Ah, here's Professor Jameson."

There are more introductions. Professor Jameson is Professor of Speech. He is not so sanguine about carrying all the luggage—it is his car. Somehow we all squeeze in.

The way to the university takes us straight through the town. It is like a thousand others in the mid-west. The main road is thirty yards broad, with a wide pavement on either side. On each side is a long low line of shops, each with big sheets of glass in their fronts, and bright Neon signs. "Eat," orders a green one; "Church of St. John," announces a deep purple; "Dance," gasps a red one; "Élite Burial Parlor," says a fourth. Through gaps between the bus station, the bank, the liquor store and the drug store, the brown prairie seems to seep in, through the small, wooden, detached residential houses behind the shops, right on to the main street. The atmosphere is one of unapologetic utilitarianism; the town looks hard, cold and spiritless; impermanent and hasty. Age has not softened it. All its history was made in a ten days' battle with the Indians, followed by fifty years of frontier vigil. Remembering, you have a sudden vision of a covered wagon on that street, and the whole place leaps into life and warmth.

"There's the campus," says Jack.

Five hundred yards ahead, the road forms a circle, about two hundred yards across. Inside it the grass looks smooth and fresh; it is planted with trees and shrubs. Around it stand the university buildings, the new-looking concrete and stuccoed walls in odd contrast with those of the town. There is the library, the art gallery, the museum, the lecture-rooms, the block of dormitories and the slim masts of the radio station. Over on the far side stands the football stadium. It is tall and U-shaped so that the light can come in at the end. The dressing-rooms are full; we hear that the bachelor ex-servicemen—the veterans—are living there; the married ones live in the cluster of "trailers" and cream-coloured hutments through which we are just passing. Over on the right is the university's airport; a few monoplanes stand glinting in the sun.

"We're putting you up at the Union," says the Professor of Speech. "It's more comfortable than any place in town." He pulls up at the centre entrance to a long high building looking like a municipal government hall. The doors are ornate, and handsome steps lead up to them. Inside, the hall is lofty; it is panelled in a light, yellowish, polished wood. A log fire burns upon a fine open hearth; the reflected light flickers on the dark leather of the saddle-back chairs. Behind the desk, where we register our names, the two young men are students, clerking part-time to pay their fees.

The following morning I stroll round the campus. It is eleven o'clock. Some hundreds of students are crossing from one lecture-room to another. They are all brightly dressed, and blithe. The boys wear trousers and lively shirts, and the girls tartan skirts and white jerseys. Some wear "blue jeans"—long blue dungarees rolled up to just below the knee—and short white socks. The boys are not all as good-looking as film stars, but they are lithe, and smart on their feet. The girls use their cosmetics with craft. Many of them have been using them since they were fourteen. They seem to bring out the individuality, not the sameness, of their features. Their hair looks free, luxuriant, vital; each hair-style seems to belong to its owner, and to no one else. They seem to have a better sense of colour than English girls who, on the other hand, have a better sense of cut. If English girls' legs are not as good, if they do not walk as well on them, they are certainly better at posing—against the rocks at Brighton or, windswept, with a golden setter. They hang much better on straps.

Young men and women walk arm-in-arm in groups or couples, over to the "coffee shop" for elevenses, or to the library, to whisper while they work. Some lie on the grass under the trees. Co-education, clearly, means far more than sitting together in class. One or two are yawning. They were out last night dancing till one a.m., and lectures this morning began as usual at eight-thirty. To miss would have been to lose some "credit."

"Did you say you wanted to see the School of Journalism?"

"If it's not inconvenient."

"Couldn't be easier. Hey! Luke! C'mon here. This is Luke Manheim, editor of the campus daily."

"This sure is a break. I've bin looking for you debaters all over. I wanted to interview you. What you think of America?"

"Wonderful."

"Say, somebody's told you. What d'you think of American women?"

"They've got jungle dignity."

"What? Say, that's good. 'Got Jungle Dignity.' That's a quote. That's good. Now is it true you've got royalty with you?"

"*What?*"

"Haven't you got a baron in the team?"

"Oh, I see. Well, yes. Edward Boyle is a baronet, that's a kind of knight——"

"Did he get that on the field of battle?"

"No. One of his ancestors was made a 'Sir' for his services to the nation, and, as it's a baronetcy, it's handed down."

"I get it. Now how should he be called? We don't know much about titles over here, but we hate to get things wrong, especially with people visitin'."

"Well, officially he's Sir Edward Boyle, but mostly on the campuses he gets called Edward or Ed."

"I get it. Now what about the Honourable Benn?"

"He's the son of a viscount——"

"You call that 'vyecount'?"

"Yes. Incidentally, in Britain it's either Mr. Benn or the Hon. A. W. Benn."

"I get it. What do Sir Edward and Mr. Benn think of your king and queen?"

"Well, er—I think, like all the British people I know, they think a great deal of them."

"Sure. I meant personally."

"You'd better ask them. I don't think they know them very well personally."

"But they're aristocrats, and the British crown rests upon the aristocracy, don't it?"

"That doesn't mean they're all in and out of Buckingham Palace all day. You only go there if you're asked."

"Uh-huh! Guess there'd be a kinda crush if it was all free. Well, here's the School of Journalism. You just go in and ask for Professor Madison. 'Jungle Dignity.' That's good. Say, what's that mean exactly?"

"Well, you know. They move along, so gracefully, and with such natural poise. Like a great cat."

"I get it. Well, I'll be seeing you."

Professor Madison was a keen young man of about thirty-five. Rocky, apparently, had been losing journalism students to other state universities. Funds and prestige had sunk together. Madison was out to re-establish Rocky's old reputation. Outlining his plans, he took me through the morgue, where clippings of the leading national newspapers were kept, past the library of books and articles on various aspects of newspapers and writing. He opened the door into one of what he called the "laboratories": about a dozen young men and women were standing at high desks, each fitting in advertisements on a dummy newspaper page. As they did so, they jotted down costs and accounts in a note-book. The first one to finish his page took it with the accounts up to the instructor. "Just like the real thing," said Madison. Next door, there was a sub-editing class. Here, the teacher was talking about how to deal with incoming news. In a kind of cupboard behind him were two Associated Press tape machines. The news was dribbling gently into a big tub. "Now supposing the editor sends down . . ." said the instructor.

But before I heard what would happen I was in the

picture library. From there we passed through the photographic plant room. "Trouble about this stuff is that it costs good money and gets broken," said Madison. He picked up a brand-new reflex camera, a shining box of tricks in black, dark blue and silver. There were six more on the shelf, and a few gross of flash-bulbs. "Good as the London *Times* gets," he said, "and any kid here can use it. Now come and see the real workshop."

We walked up the corridor, and pushed past two baize-covered doors. We were in a complete printing works. Along one side ran a shining press, of about the size that an up-to-date county newspaper would be using. There were Linotype machines, compositors' stones, even a furnace for melting down the lead. The students worked the plant, supervised by the expert printer, aided by a man to work the lead.

"Everybody looks pretty busy," I said.

"Certainly they are. They bring a paper out every day. Four thousand circulation."

"Who pays for it?"

"We try and make it pay for itself. It sells for a couple of cents, and we get plenty of ads."

"Are these people working here doing it spare time or academically?"

"Academically, you might say. They get credit for it, anyway. Now you want to go over to the radio station." He looked round the room at the busy figures. "I've got to take a class on 'Interviewing,'" he said. "I'll get one of the boys to take you over. Bill, will you take this gentleman over to the radio shop?"

"Why sure, Professor."

We walked round the campus circle towards the radio masts. "So you're going to be a journalist, Bill?"

"Oh, no," he said. "I'm going on studying English literature. In order to major——"

"'What's 'major'?"

"Well, I suppose it's your bachelor's degree. To get it I've also got to get credit in two other subsidiary subjects. So I'm putting in thirteen hours on journalism and thirteen on music."

"Hours?"

"Yeah. That's how you get credit, putting in so many hours."

"But don't you get an examination?"

"Examination! I'm telling *you* we get examinations."

"But not one big one, what we call finals, at the end of two or three years?"

"No. We do ours in sections, a bit at a time, spread out over whatever the period is—two or three years maybe."

"As far as 'majoring' is concerned then, you can forget what you've learned as soon as you've passed the section."

"Sure. But you don't want to forget it. It's all so interesting and *useful*."

At the radio station vestibule we met Herb Cantello. Half his time he spent as programme controller, the other half as a post-graduate student working on his Master's thesis. First we saw the gramophone library where two student "disc-jockeys" were preparing for a thirty-minute recital, and another was busy cataloguing. Then we looked in at a small studio where a girl was reading a newscast. When she had finished, a young man came forward and delivered a lyrical advertisement for a local firm.

"Damn it," I said. "I'd have thought the university radio station could have kept its programme uncommercial."

"But why?" he said. "The fees we get from them

make it possible for us to put on the music and the talks. Besides, it's what happens on the air outside. Our students don't get any illusions about what keeps culture on the air."

Through an elaborately equipped sound-effects room we came into a small auditorium. About a hundred desks were arranged in sharply ascending tiers. In the front was a rostrum. Behind this was a large plate-glass window. On the inside it had thick curtains which could be pulled by a cord. When the window was uncovered the auditorium looked into the main studio. There was a two-way radio system connecting them. "Demonstration room," said Herb; "programme goes out from main studio. Class sits and looks on. Professor pulls the hell out of it."

"Do you take much interest in the British Broadcasting Corporation here?"

"Yes, a certain amount."

"What do people think about it?"

"Our students think a great deal of a service which doesn't have to get mixed up with commercials. And they know what a high level of entertainment it hits compared to ours. But those who were over there and heard it, well, they figured it was a bit dull."

"What do you think of the Third Programme?"

"Never heard of it." I explained. "Gee! That sounds pretty good. That's really revolutionary!"

He walked with me to the door. Two men were coming in. One was the Professor of Economics, and the other was one of the State's leading Congressmen. They were going to have a broadcast battle on the subject of price-controls. "That reminds me," said Herb, "I'd have been seeing you and your two friends to-night anyway. At the discussion."

"Discussion?"

"Yes. In the main studio there. With the Rocky debaters at seven o'clock. Going out on the State network."

"But that's the first I've heard of this! What on earth are we going to talk about? Where's the script?"

"We don't want to hear you boys read. We want to hear you talk."

"Good Lord!"

"That'll be O.K. You'll enjoy it. You know, that Congressman of ours is going to have his tail twisted this afternoon by Professor Davies, but he'll put up with it. He doesn't get a script either."

Outside, I stood in the sun for a moment feeling a little dazed. Suddenly there was a light musical hail. "Hullo there! Oxford!" A young lady was walking along the opposite side of the road. She wore a flowing red cloak. Her hair was like smooth pale gold, and her eyes as blue as the English cornflower.

"I wanted to tell you boys how much I enjoyed that debate last night," she said. She had the American girl's knack of looking at you as though you really mattered. "You boys aren't at a loss for a word, are you?"

"We boys are going to be at a loss for one to-night," I said. "We've got to take part in an impromptu discussion without a script."

"What d'you think of American radio?"

"Well, I've heard some of these fifteen-minute love and suffering serials, these—er——"

"Soap operas?"

"Yes. And I must say I think they're pretty frightful."

"They're meant for just some listeners. Plenty of other stations on the dial."

"Pah! I can't think who can listen to such awful tripe."

"Chiefly women. Women who look after the house. It's not much fun, with your husband at work all day, and the kids at school, and the dishes to wash and the clothes to mend. They get lonely and tired——"

"Tired, with electric mangles? Lonely, with a thousand people living in the same block?"

"Say, why don't you come out of New York? That's the trouble with you British. You come out here, all of you, lecturers, painters and singers and writers, and you either stay on the east coast, or hop right over to California. Or you stay in Britain, complain that Hollywood films are far-fetched, and swallow them whole. Everybody's rich out here, and everybody listens to soap operas. We get it both ways."

"Sorry."

"Oh, well; I guess we swallow it too." She looked at her watch. "Where are you going now?"

"Nowhere special," I said. "Where are you going?"

"I'm going to a drama class. Want to come?"

"Yes please."

"C'mon."

The theatre stood outside the rim of the campus circle. We walked about a quarter of a mile down a side-road to get to it. It was built of pale-coloured brick. One side bulged out into a big wing. It held the properties. Above the stage end, the roof rose sharply to make a great cage for the drops and the back-cloths. We passed by the gilded portals and ironwork flambeaux of the main entrance, and entered by a side door.

"Want to see around first?"

"Please."

The stage was as big as the one or two I saw in New York. Practically the whole of it was on the circular piece which revolved at the touch of an electric button. Including the wing, there was more room behind than in front of the proscenium arch. About six hundred people could sit comfortably in the plush armchairs which were set on a steeply rising ramp. The stage and house lighting was more elaborate than anything I had ever seen outside a West End theatre. Every light was controlled from a small, compact, desk-top switchboard in the soundproof room behind the back row of the stalls. It was the kind of theatre that is a producer's dream. And it was for students.

"It's magnificent. What play are you putting on next?"

"*Dracula.*"

"H'm."

"Don't say it. I know. They wanted to do something low-brow for a change. C'mon. Let's have a quick peek behind."

Under the auditorium were a number of rehearsing studios. Stirring lines from *Henry V* resounded from behind a half-open door, and as we walked on down the corridor my ear caught the hollow groan of a Greek chorus. From another door came an even more familiar sound. "Well!" I said. "I've only been to a few universities so far, but this is the fourth one to be putting on *The Importance of Being Earnest.*"

"It's got everything we haven't got."

The drama class was held in the Green Room. We sat back in basketwork chairs and smoked cigarettes. There were about twenty boys and girls there, sitting on the floor, perched on the furniture or leaning back in the chairs. At length the instructor appeared. He was about thirty. Everybody called him "Huck." He wore a pretty shirt which, he told us, had once been a Japanese girl's kimono. He told us how the kimono had become a shirt. He was a charming raconteur, and a very pleasant personality.

"Well," he said. "Let's get to work."

We were going to discuss the production difficulties of *The Importance*. "Now, first of all, let's talk about its qualities," he said. "What would we aim to bring out?" We had a long discussion. Eventually we decided we would aim first to bring out the Englishness of it. Then its humour, its elegance, and its sophistication.

"Huck," said a boy, thoughtfully, suddenly looking up from his note-book. "Stylization. Would that be a good word to use about it, Huck?"

We moved on to the casting of the play. "First, let's cast it in terms of personalities in this class," said Huck. We did this. "Now people we know on the campus. . . . Now, film stars."

An hour went by very agreeably. Around me the girls and boys had garnered a rich harvest of notes. Huck brightened his instruction with anecdotes and illustrations drawn from his experiences in Hollywood and Broadway. "Now, something to work on for next time," he wound up. "Choose a scene from *The Importance*. Make your production notes on it—choose your furniture, the setting, and sketch out the movements. O.K.?"

"O.K., Huck."

The girl in the red cloak guided me back to the Union. "Now you're ready to start producing on Broadway," I said.

"If I wanted to be a prodoocer," she answered, "I'd learn on the boards."

"What *do* you want to do?"

"Be a nurse."

"Well why on earth do you want to know what furniture to use for a play?"

"Can't nurses know something about the theatre?"

"Of course. But they can pick that kind of thing up as they go along."

"Go along where?"

"Well, where they work or where they live."

"Where they live. See here, I'm a farmer's daughter. I live right out in the prairie, three hundred miles from here. When I'm at home, I don't see twenty people my own age from one year's end to another. And you say I can pick up something about the theatre. I don't come in here to fill my head with book stuff mainly. I come in to meet people, and to live a bit. Huck, now. He's been to Hollywood, and he's been on Broadway. He wasn't great shakes there, but he was *there*. Talking and listening to him's as near as I'll ever get. In England, I guess, you can't be farther than a couple of hundred miles from London wherever you live. Over here you can be a couple of hundred miles from the nearest town. It's the people who don't understand that who find education over here so comic."

"I don't think anybody finds it comic."

"You people from England do."

"Well, all right," I said, "we do. And it's up to you to tell us why we shouldn't."

"Well, you take my aunt. She lived out in the prairie with my uncle, almost on her own for fifteen years, having children and helping him on the farm in the bad times. D'you know the first thing she wanted to do when the littlest kid was raised and my uncle had enough money for her to quit working herself to death?"

"No."

"She wanted to go into town, twice a week, drive sixty-five miles in and sixty-five miles out, to take lessons —in musical appreciation."

"What did your uncle say?"

"He said she was crazy."

"Well, quite frankly, I think she was."

"Maybe. But it isn't important whether she was

crazy or not. What's important is whether she really wanted to do it, or whether she did it just to show off. I can tell you: she was dead serious about it. When you people criticize the things we do to get educated, you forget that we're dead serious too, as serious as any of those monks or friars or whatever they were, that got your universities started."

We got to the door of the Union. "Here you are then, Oxford," said the girl.

"Here we are then," I said. "There's one thing you can be sure of. When I get home to Britain, if there's one thing I'll bear witness to, it's that Americans take education pretty seriously."

"That's right. And that doesn't mean we gotta put on gowns and say the grace in Latin. O.K.?"

"O.K."

That night I sat in the rooms of Professor Arthur Y. Westinghouse. The "Professor" and the "Arthur Y." meant nothing to me. We had been up together at Oxford before the war, and as far as I was concerned he was still "Barney." "Have a look at this, Barney," I said. In front of him I put the following account:

"In Britain, one person in a thousand is at college or university: in America, one in seventy. This is not only because the Americans can afford to spend more money on education than we can—they can afford to spend more money on their back-gardens, but don't—but because their view of education is different from ours. Their society being still so young, nature being so dangerous as well as bountiful, there are always a thousand urgent tasks, mental and physical, to be done. The hands and minds to tackle them will be trained at the university. This is why, at so many of them, you can take a course in anything from Egyptology to hotel management; why one treatise is written on the 'Publishing Trade in Fifteenth-Century London,' and another on 'Eighteen Ways of Washing Dishes.'"

"Even to-day, when they may be serving far more Arts than Science students, some of the largest universities and colleges look back to the days when they were created to teach engineering and agriculture. Then, building machines and coaxing crops from the virgin soil were more pressing needs than seminars for philosophy. The vocational approach is still strong: subjects are often treated as techniques to be mastered rather than as intellectual or æsthetic experiences to be understood and lived through: history, philosophy and literature seem sometimes to be taught in the scientific, formal, tabloid lay-out of a book on 'How to Grow Tomatoes.'

"All other aspects of the American's attitude to education are overshadowed by one: his unbounded faith in it. In Britain, many self-made men, business men and adventurers, will often ask 'What is the point of a university?' and say that they believe in boys being pitched out to learn in the hard school of the world as soon as possible. You never hear that kind of remark in the United States. Millions of business men and women, who might otherwise have been 'self-made,' take part-time courses, go to night school, until late in life. There is a great respect for the university, from the tycoon down to the taxi-cab driver. Perhaps it is because they are so confident that their universities are 'useful,' and because so much of the 'hard school of the world' has been caught, tamed and forced into text-books, and taught in the class and lecture-room."

"Yes," he said, "that's all quite true."

"But the thing that gets in so many gizzards," I said, "is that you're so keen, over here, on educating everybody, that the standard of education enjoyed by any one person is bound to be pretty low."

"Pretty low compared to what?"

"Well, say, to what he'd get at a place where each pupil had far more time and attention devoted to him personally, but where there are far fewer pupils. The few being selected by competition; scholarships, and so on."

"Well," said Barney, "you've always had an aristocratic tradition running through your educational system. First, the well-born people went to Oxford and Cambridge, then, as democratic ideas became more efficient, that handful of aristocratic vacancies became available through open competition; and so on, through the newer universities. But over here, we had to deal with the masses almost from the start. And our educationalists came into a society which had already made up its mind that whatever was going ought to be shared out equally all round. You might say that we care more for the equality of the product than we care for its class."

"Do you really believe in the American type of education, Barney?"

"I don't know. But I'm sure of one thing, which is that the answer to our problem can't be imported from Britain. Or from Germany, or from France. That's the mistake we've made in the past. We forgot that when people started building Oxford in the thirteenth century they didn't have any blue-print, any 'The Ideal of a University' to work from."

"What're you getting at?"

"This. I think education in America may want a tremendous amount of thought, and a lot of criticism. But it shouldn't be criticized in terms of standards and methods which have been successful in other kinds of community. Not unless the community is like ours.

It's when we copy you we look foolish. Evelyn Waugh or Eric Linklater can come over here and make a mid-west university look like a burlesque show. Though as a matter of fact, James Thurber could do the same for Oxford. Anyway, a community gets the kind of university it deserves and needs in the long run. And I suppose we'll hammer out our deserts and needs in time too."

"If you don't mind my saying so," I said, "I think your people deserve and need better than they've got at present."

"You're right," he said. "Well, we'll hope for the best; for leadership, and the right people to come and teach."

I looked out of the window to where the little ring of culture ended, and the vast plain began again; on all sides, like a sea. "By the way," I said. "When you came down from Oxford, you said you were going into business."

"That's right. I went into business, at that."

"Didn't you like it?"

"Sure I liked it. Very much. It was just that I thought I'd like teaching more."

"Why didn't you stay on the east coast?"

"Well," said Barney, looking in his turn out of the window, "I guess there were two reasons. First, I thought a spell out here in the sticks would give me a chance to find out how much I learned at Oxford was the real M'Coy. Second . . . well . . . if it hadn't been for this particular university popping up on the prairie I don't suppose I'd have got to Oxford at all. I'd have been punching cows a hundred miles down the line."

He looked at his watch. "Time you went," he said. "Your train leaves at eight to-morrow."

I got up to go. "There's one thing about it, Barney," I said. "You Americans do *believe* in education."

"Yes," he said. "We do. We always have believed in it. And now that we can see the new tasks and responsibilities we've got to take up in the world, well, I guess we believe in it, and hope from it, a great deal more."

He got up and crossed to the door where his Oxford B.A. hood hung on a hook. He took down the broad-brimmed Stetson which made him look more like a farmer than a don and put it on.

"I guess we'd better leave it at that for now," he said. "Let's go."

CHAPTER VII

Americans Hit the Road

An American can leave New York, fly twice the distance from London to Moscow, and find himself still in his own country.

Even those people who do not leave New York can get an idea of distance in the United States. The railway train speaks of it, as it stands humming and hissing in the station. It lacks the characteristic shape of the British engine, the long round belly of a boiler, the stunted funnel, the tall broad-spoked wheels. The American locomotive is a great long metal box, the engineers walking round the diesel units inside like electricians in a power-house. On the platforms, signboards show where each train is bound for: this one to Chicago—1,000 miles, this one to Miami—1,400 miles, and that one, over there, ready to start its passengers on the 2,500 mile stretch across to the west coast.

Travel by train is more of a campaign than an assault. Security, comfort and sure arrival, rather than speed, are the main features of the arrangements. Wealthier passengers take "drawing-rooms," containing two or three bunks, a sofa and a lavatory. They take their radio set and typewriter with them. There are compartments which are comfortable coaches by day and shadowy, green-curtained sleeping-shelves by night. There is the ordinary coach where, if you can grab a double seat for yourself, adjust the seat and the foot-rests and hire a pillow, you can sleep in comfort. At stations, a little band of functionaries will come on board, like islanders coming out to a passing ship. The "Butch" sells milk, coffee, fruit, sandwiches, and chocolate from a big basket. Another man sells newspapers and books, and a third comes round to deliver or collect telegrams. The business man sitting opposite you is sending another cable: he may have done three or four business deals by the time he gets off this train. Last night, you recall, people boarding the train wore overcoats. This morning, new passengers are wearing panamas and open-necked shirts. Along this fifteen-hundred-mile descent from north to south, the train drops through different climates like an elevator through the different floors.

A glance at an airport shows this even more vividly. La Guardia, one of New York's two big flying-fields, is a national and an international hub. Two-engined aircraft are taking off every few minutes to fly, at about a pound a hundred miles, to nearly every fair-sized town in the east. Bigger two-engined planes are flying to Chicago in three or four hours. Now and again a four-engined giant sweeps in from San Francisco, the Pacific Islands, or from Europe. Travellers to and from three continents get in and out of planes as casually as if they were crossing a county, not a world. They stand chatting in the airport vestibule, men carrying fur coats rubbing shoulders with men wearing linen jackets.

People write in the same slang, and mail the letter for three cents, to relatives and friends a thousand miles across country. Children go to their grandmother's funeral by airplane. Students thumb a lift across a continent for the Christmas holidays. Trips into Canada, vacations in the West Indies, hang like scalps at the money-belt of those who have a couple of hundred dollars a year to spare. There are still millions of Americans who have never been out of town; but the present wave of prosperity has borne millions more into mountains and forests miles away from their homes.

All this combines to form the present attitude of the American to the matter of getting from one place to another at any time. There is only one word for it, and the word is casual. They take distance in their stride. It does not worry them.

One morning we left Peoria by air for Chicago. We were due to arrive there at noon, in order to catch another plane to get us to Madison, in Wisconsin, in time to debate at eight p.m. We were late, and the connecting plane went off without us. We explained our predicament to the young ladies at the desk. They listened with a sympathetic but calm air. When they turned to their time-tables for a substitute route, their manner was unhurried. They were used to routing the unconnected over a continent. They discovered quite quickly that if we flew to City A, we could catch a train to City B. Thence a bus would take us to Madison, where, with luck, we would be ready to debate at eight-thirty.

At that point one of us remembered that we had made a promise on the boat to ring up Professor Cleaver of Chicago University if we ever passed near. (Just to say "Hullo!") While Edward Boyle and I marshalled the suit-cases, Wedgwood Benn went to the telephone box. In a few minutes he was back, looking rather bewildered. "Cleaver says there's no point in messing about with buses and trains," he said. "He says he'll come up with his car and drive us to Madison."

"He can't possibly do that," I said. "It's more than five hours' driving. And he'll have to come back on his own."

"And what about his classes?" said Edward.

"He's not lecturing till noon to-morrow, and he says

he can get back by then," said Anthony. "In any case, there's no point in us arguing. He's on his way here."

Cleaver arrived in about twenty minutes. He was wearing an old suit and a floppy hat. He looked as though he might have just come from mowing the lawn. His luggage consisted of a large paper bag in which his wife had hastily packed fruit and sandwiches. "O.K., boys," he said. "Jump in."

We drove steadily up the 200-mile stretch to Madison. "You boys rest your voices for to-night," said Cleaver. "I'll talk till you tell me to hush up." We talked chiefly about Socialism in America, and the question of how to reconcile what was going on in Britain with the old Liberal ideas of individual freedom. "All very well you British saying we Yanks don't know how tough things are, and how much freedom has to be sacrified because of an emergency. But you don't verbalize enough about what you're doing. You don't explain."

We arrived at Madison at seven. After a quick wash we marched into the Union restaurant where our hosts were waiting for us. "This is Professor Cleaver," we said. "He's brought us all the way from Chicago, otherwise we'd never have got here."

"Why, thanks, Cleaver," said the Professor of Speech. He sounded very grateful, but not at all surprised. As for Cleaver, he had already seated himself and plunged into a conversation about Marshall Aid.

At quarter to eight we all got up to go to the debating hall. We heard Cleaver say that since he would be getting up before dawn next morning, he had better go early to bed. "Well, good-bye, Professor," we said. "And thank you again."

The Professor stood for a moment in thought. "On second thoughts," he said, "I might just as well stay and hear you boys shoot."

All through the debate we could see his spectacles gleaming cheerfully in the gallery. It was like having an old friend up there. Afterwards he was pressed into joining a small party given by the Professor of Speech. "Well, O.K.," he said. "As long as I get to bed pretty soon." But at midnight he was on the station platform seeing us off to our next university. "You boys get into your bunks right away," he said. "Talking all the time, you need plenty of sleep."

* * * * *

On a lovely day in the Canadian fall, we were being given lunch at the University of Toronto. "You must see the Niagara Falls," said our hosts. "The American side looks bigger, but more water goes over ours."

"We'd love to," we said. "But we've got to be in New York to-morrow morning, and the trains are very tricky."

There was some whispering across the tables for the rest of the meal, and a little semaphore up and down the room. "We've got two cars fixed up," said one of the faculty members as soon as the meal was over. "If we leave by four, we'll get there soon after six."

We arrived at the falls by six, having driven just under a hundred miles. When we got there one of the cars broke down. While it was being mended we had a very merry dinner-party. At nine o'clock the car appeared. We prepared to leave—the Oxford men to catch the train to Buffalo; the Canadians, we imagined, to drive back home.

"Good-bye," we said.

"Good-bye nothing," they said. "We're driving you boys over to Buffalo."

We drove the twenty-two miles to Buffalo. The

Canadians waited till our train came in at eleven-thirty, and then began the five-hour drive to Toronto. Three of them were due in the office at eight-thirty the following morning. When we heard this we clucked sympathetically; they stared at us as if they did not understand. I was never with eight people who seemed to get on better together, and in the train I said so to Anthony. "I thought the same thing myself," he said. "But one of them told me that he and his wife had never met any of the others before, and I know that those two girls have only been in the place a week."

* * * * *

Mitchelmore College was the one place we visited twice. We left it for the first time on a Friday morning. It was a sad parting. "You must come back," they said.

"We'd love to."

"Well, why don't you?"

"We've got to debate at Surrey to-night."

"You can come back to-morrow."

"Well," we said. "If Surrey aren't expecting us to stay the week-end, we'll come back and spend it with you. That is, if we can get a train."

"O.K. If the trains aren't too good, we'll come halfway and fetch you. Call us up to-night and tell us what's happening. O.K.?"

"O.K."

We got to Surrey. We gathered that the week-end was our own. Just before the debate began, we rang up Mitchelmore to say that we would be coming over next day, and would wire when we knew what train we could catch.

The debate finished at ten. There was a variety show going on in a hall on the other side of the campus, and the debating squad escorted us over to see it. The show lasted till eleven. As the final applause died down, I looked around for my two colleagues. Just then I felt a tap on the shoulder. "Well, here's one of you, anyway," said a voice. I turned and saw an American debater standing in front of me. "Ready?" he said.

"For what?"

"Why, to go."

"Oh, don't you bother," I said. "We can find our own way down to the hotel."

"Might as well go in the car," he said. "I suppose you've all packed?"

"*Packed?*" I said. "Hell, we've only just *un*-packed. We needn't pack till morning."

"Hell, too," he said. "You're gonna be back in Mitchelmore by morning."

It then dawned on me that he was a debater from Mitchelmore, not Surrey. It seemed that he happened to have been in the Speech Office when our telephone message came through. As he "wasn't doing anything much that evening," he thought he might as well come over and collect us right away. "We'll be there for sure by three," he said.

"But wasn't it lonely, Johnny, driving one hundred and twenty miles at this time of night?"

"No," he said. "I brought the wife."

There she was, out in the big, battered car—fluffy-haired, bright-eyed, as fresh and lively as though she were bound for a cocktail-party. Husband and wife and a debater squeezed into the front, two debaters and nine suit-cases crammed into the back, and off we roared at eleven-thirty along the straight prairie road. At one in the morning we stopped at a roadside drug store and ate hot dogs washed down with coffee. For the next thirty miles our driver sang sweet, haunting, cowboy songs about cattle on the skyline and faithful ponies. The wife stayed awake, throwing away one and then lighting another cigarette for the man at the wheel. The Oxford debaters fell asleep.

That week-end at Mitchelmore was unforgettable. The second parting was even more sad than the first, except that having returned once we began to feel that no parting need be final. On the Sunday, to make sure that we had time to stay for lunch, instead of putting us on the noon train the young Professor of Speech insisted on driving us to our next destination. It was 150 miles away.

In the hotel at which he left us, we said good-bye. It was late, and we were a little worried about him. "I just don't know what you boys are fussing about," he said. And his face showed that he didn't. "I'm fine," he repeated. "I'll just call my wife and tell her how things are going."

He went to the telephone in the hall, and picked up the receiver. "Is that you, honey?" we heard him say in a few moments. "Yes. A swell trip, too. Now see here; being I'm over this far, I might as well go round by Beltonville and look up your Ma. It's only a few miles out. I'll be in about four. O.K.?"

"O.K." we heard faintly from the other end. And O.K. it seemed to be.

The American's casual attitude to travel gives the European visitor the feeling that he has been brought up under a tub. Professor Smith has just gone to Honolulu to give a memorial lecture. The boy next door has gone a thousand miles to sell a hundredweight of paint. Johnny across the street is motoring four hundred miles to be best man at his cousin's wedding. Here lives and multiplies a people with a real world-sense. It does not come out of a religion preaching the brotherhood of man, nor from an economic theory of his interdependence. It grows naturally out of the big broad land in which the Americans live. They inhabit a world, not a country. This is why they learned so soon the technique of a global war. It should make them leaders in a global peace.

CHAPTER VIII

Americans at Home

No door is more open to the stranger than the American's. This is true of him whether he is a well-rooted Mid-western descendant of an Anglo-Saxon family or a first-generation Hungarian on the edge of Manhattan. It may be the handed-down memory of the frontier days which makes it so, or reaction from those first few days on the bleak unfriendly beaches of a new world. Certainly the size of the country keeps the heart of entertainment warm. Whatever the cause, the door is always open.

The first American home I stayed at was half an hour across the Hudson river from New York. I went over by bus. "Here it is, bud. Melville," said the driver-conductor. He gave me some change from the tiny cash register on his belt, and, without leaving his seat, pulled the lever which automatically opened the door. "Where d'you want to get to?"

"Lincoln Avenue."

"Up there; go past the funeral parlour and the bank. Turn left when you see No. 17 school——"

"Number what?"

"No. 17 school. Schools here have numbers, not names. Hope you find it O.K."

The bus, long and narrow, hissed off round the corner. I began to walk up the hill. All the houses seemed built of wood, white or light-coloured timber in over-lapping planks set parallel to the ground. Most of them were a step or two up from the ground, with a veranda in front. Their steep roofs, the high gables and the white wood, made them look Scandinavian rather than British. Each stood back from the asphalt pavement and away from the others, at regular intervals along straight streets. From the air it must have looked like an army camp.

"Excuse me. But am I going right for Lincoln Avenue?"

"Sure. Cross over by the Pantarium and——"

"What's the Pantarium?"

"Where you get your trousers pressed. While you wait."

Each house had its own plot of ground. There was full scope for privacy, but this community of individualists seemed to prefer not to take it. Though there were variations in their design they had one thing in common: there were no hedges or fences between them, and no wall to part them from the pavement. Children and dogs ran without let from one front to another. Along the kerbs of the side-streets were green strips of turf and an occasional tree in blossom. But there were few lawns and few flower-gardens. Not even a window-box seemed to challenge the encroaching city. The good people of Melville had delegated their gardening to the local government. In the Welsh valleys, rising from the coal-dust, and in the Lancashire towns, shining through the mists that keep the cotton damp, the bowl of hyacinths, the tiny lawn, the straggling runner bean, proclaim that the industrial worker still feels the call of the soil. The Americans are great landsmen; but once they leave the farm they seem ready to leave it for good.

The first American door opened to me. "C'mon in," they said, as a hundred other families were to say in the same welcoming voice. As I was to do on dozens of occasions all over the country, I took off my coat and hung it on a coat-hanger, not a hook. "Sit down," they said. They didn't have to say "Make yourself at home." They hung up your shyness for you with your hat.

An American meal is a medley of the food of two worlds. Frankfurter sausages from Europe, but packed in American nylon. Hamburger steaks, but coming from the butcher in round, hard discs which rattle like quoits as they drop in the pan. Beer tasting like Lager, but poured from a can looking as though it held bicycle oil. Old World water, tinkling and sparkling in ice-filled long-barrelled tumblers. White bread, soft-crusted, and delivered already sliced. A side-plate of lettuces, with mayonnaise, cream cheese and a peach in the centre, to eat between courses. Ice-cream with the sweet. In some houses, we ate no butter: it was five shillings a pound. The margarine was colourless till, without taking off the cellophane wrapper, the hostess kneaded from one corner of it a blob of brown dye. In a moment or two the whole was a rich, yolky yellow.

In Meadowville, Jim Wilson, a big, bald, perspiring bank-manager, asked me round to supper. "C'mon in," he said. He was in his shirt sleeves, his trousers held up by tags at the hip. "Kind of warm. Take off your jacket." I took off my coat. "What d'you wear suspenders for?" he asked. He looked at my braces as though I was displaying some piece of intimate medical apparatus. "What d'you think of this house of mine? I've just had it built."

I looked around. One end of the very large room on the ground floor was made into a recess by two short protruding pieces on opposite walls. From the recess, in which stood a dining-table and chairs, an arch led into a tiny writing-room, and a swing-door into a large airy kitchen-breakfast-room. The front door led straight from the big room out on to the fly-netted veranda. There was no hall. The stairs rose from just inside the door to the first floor—second floor in America—where there were two large bedrooms, two small ones and a bathroom. "It's very well designed," I said.

"What kind of a house would someone like me have in England?"

"Well, in England," I said, "however small the place is, we try and make it into separate rooms with a door to each."

"Why?"

"Well, I suppose we like having a number of separate rooms, and each one being shut off. Privacy, you know."

"You can have the privacy. Give me convenience. If I want to be private, I reckon I can go to bed."

Not till I had passed through another twenty-five states did I see a house which might have been built in Britain. It was a country house in South Carolina, square and solid-looking, with thick stone walls and small lofty rooms. Everywhere there were doors which we opened and shut as though shaking hands with old friends. Elsewhere even the houses of the rich were divided on the ground floor into a number of rooms, all opening through wide arches into the centre hall. From the front door you could see and hear what was going on in every room.

When central heating is a common feature, doors do not become as necessary as they do when every room has to guard its fire's heat jealously. Quite modest American houses have an oil-furnace in the cellar, sending the hot air through concealed chimneys or swirling up through gratings in the floor. The absence of a fire gives many an American room an unfamiliar look to the British visitor. Though there may be a fireplace, the room does not look towards it. The easy chairs do not face it, the pipe-rack and the favourite book-case are not handy by its side. The furniture seems often to face all ways or no ways. To an Englishman who had not realized how the fireplace had dominated his unconscious mind, the aspect of American rooms was comfortable but never cosy. Americans love their homes; but they seem not to have our feeling for the hearth.

"So you think we Americans love our homes, do you?" said one American.

"Yes, I think so."

"I'm not sure. Seems to me we're always trying to get out of them. Clubs, theatres, ice-rink, films, sports, parties. And not just entertainments, you understand. Evening school, voluntary services, helping with the Church work, running charity drives. All we seem to use the home for's to eat, sleep and keep our clothes. It's not that we're just doing it for fun, you understand. It's just because we kind of like getting together. We're matey. Ah, well, I guess human beings weren't meant to be alone anyway."

"I don't call being home with the family 'being alone.'"

"No. Sure. I guess some of you British think even that's a crowd. I knew a guy in London who used to go out of the house to get some solitude, he said."

When the American does go out for the evening, he seems able to stay out later and enjoy himself more thoroughly than most British people would. Whether it is because of a richer, meatier diet, more physical energy, a drier atmosphere, or just the American way of life, he seems to manage on far less sleep. Going to bed and getting up at routine times does not seem to matter to him. Like the animal, he lies down when he is tired, and gets up when there is something to be done. It seems to do him no harm, though under the eyes and round the mouths of American boys and girls of twenty are often lines and shadows which super-fatted cosmetics and after-shaving lotion don't conceal.

To cope with the Americans' late-night needs and desires, entertainments, restaurants and hotels work pretty late. Our first breakdown in schedule landed us in a fair-sized mid-west town, unheralded and unbooked, at a few minutes before midnight. As we lugged our suit-cases off the train, our hearts were low at the prospect of sleeping on benches without any chance of supper. When we got into the station vestibule, our spirits rose. People were getting off and on to trains as though it were twelve noon. Restaurants were steaming and hissing with frying eggs and bacon, and humming with the conversation of travellers. We ascended to the hotel. The vestibule blazed with lights, and the reception desk bustled with activity. In the lounge people sat around and drank cocktails, the sounds of exciting dance music and energetic feet floated down the long corridor to the hall. The main doors opened and in came another dozen or so people, talking and laughing. Their bright faces and high tones suggested that the evening was just beginning for them. The light, the laughter, the music, infected us with a sense that it was almost beginning for us.

A boy stood near me while his girl deposited her coat. "Is there a dance here?" I said.

"Yeah."

"It sounds very gay."

"Think so? Ordinary supper dance."

"D'you mean it's like this every night?"

"Sure."

"Well," I said. "I don't know how you Americans can do it."

"Do what?"

"Stay up so late every night."

"We don't. Me, f'rinstance. I'll be up till two or

three to-night, but to-morrow I'll go to bed early. I'll be in bed by twelve, latest."

One of the things British people miss in the United States is the village inn. In the big towns there are expensive, smoothly got up cocktail bars, and the small towns have their liquor shops or bars. But on the whole, apart from the lounge in some hotels there is nothing in between. The American does not walk round to the local two or three times a week with his wife or with his son, to have his pint, his chat with the neighbours, and then his walk home. He does not take out the dog last thing every night, and break his journey with a quick one at The Crown. He either goes out on a flashy binge with a party at a cocktail lounge or has a really good soak with "the boys." Drinking in America outside private houses is, on the whole, a raw business, and the regular drinker in the city bars, when he has had a few, is more likely to say something rude than to sing a song. Over there less women seemed to drink than here. But those that did seemed to leave off rather later than British women.

One of the things that the Britisher has to get used to is the patches of Prohibition with which the country is still dappled. When the whole state is officially dry, like Kansas, one knows where one is. But when one county, or town, is dry and the next is not it becomes confusing. One hot day I got into a taxi in a town in Florida. "English?" said the driver.

"That's right."

"Bet you miss that beer of yours down here."

"I certainly do. Still, I'll get a bottle of lager at the hotel."

"Oh no you won't."

"Not even that canned stuff?"

"Not even that canned stuff. This place's dry as dust."

"But I didn't know Florida was a dry state!"

"It ain't. We gotta local option. We voted, and the vote said 'Dry.' You'll have to have a chocolate soda."

"Might it ever change to wet?"

"Naw. What's the point? The teetot'lers like it as it is; the liquor-sluggers drive five miles down the road to the next county and load up with a case or two. Everybody's happy."

Some towns, though "dry," sold bottled beer as freely as Coca-cola. In others you could buy "hard" liquor in one of the State-controlled "liquor" shops if you had the necessary official "liquor-book." In South Carolina I could not buy anything but beer across the hotel bar; but if I brought in a bottle of whisky or gin, as some of the residents did, the barman would make it up into cocktails for me, or sell me soda to drink with it.

"A man who could tell you just what you could and couldn't do for a drink in every state," said Tom Brown, an Englishman who'd been fifteen years in America, "would have to be a walking encyclopædia."

"You've seen both countries," I said. "Don't you think that British people use drink more than the Americans do to get 'eased up,' get a party warmed up, and that kind of a thing?"

"Yes," he said. "They don't need much priming over here. They start off warm. Last night, now. Half a dozen of our neighbours came in. We had a thoroughly gay time on a cup of cocoa with a marshmallow in it."

"You know, Tom," I said. "In my first few days over here some of the people were so easy to get on with, so cheery and forward, I thought they must have been drinking."

"Cocoa with a marshmallow," said Tom. "*I* noticed this friendliness, this unself-consciousness among the neighbours when *I* came over." He looked out of the window at the comfortable, double-decked, detached houses across the street. "Now take this place, for instance. In Britain, you'd call it a middle-class—perhaps a lower middle-class—residential area. You know, bank clerks, secondary schoolmasters, lawyers, doctors and so on. Now back where I lived in England, in a similar kind of background, people were very cut off. They called on each other, and that kind of thing, but they weren't really matey. They put up a little screen of discretion around all their goings out and their comings in. The only thing they were prepared to have their neighbours know was their success. Now over here the neighbours come busting in on your failures as well. They come and give you a meal when they hear the wife is sick; they come and help you mend the car. If they hear you're not doing well and you're thinking of going to live in some other part, they come in and tell you what they think."

"Do you like it that way?"

"Well, if you stay here, you've got to have it that way. It'd drive many an Englishman I know crazy. But his children'd do better on it than they would back there."

All the American's casualness and kindness comes out in the way he treats his children. All his optimism, his belief in human nature, his hope for the future of the man next door, go into the freedom and trust he gives them. For him, they seem to be not *his*, but so many other individual members of the family. He does not believe that they should be seen and not heard. As soon as they are big enough they sit at table. They horn in on the conversation almost as soon as they can talk. In one house, a little boy next to me was interrupting every two minutes. "Junior," said his mother at last, "for Pete's sake give your father a chance." The children I met looked at me solemnly but not shyly. They were polite, but once they had heard it, they called me by my Christian name. It was "Ciss" and "Tom," not "Auntie Ciss" or "Uncle Tom," and I heard lots of children call their parents by their Christian or by some family name. American children are more mature than ours are, though in an engaging, not a precocious kind of way. They talk better and more freely earlier on. They do not suck their thumbs and they cry less. If they want to show off they don't stand twisting their dresses in their fingers while their parents coax them to recite some little poem. They go and ride like mad on a tricycle in the garden.

"It's the ruin of our education," said the High School headmaster, as we stood in the school-yard at "break."

"What is?"

"The things we do for our children."

"Sounds funny."

"We make things too pleasant for them. We reckon that children have got to have a good time. They've got to grow up with a good memory of being young. Not too many text-books, not too many hard lessons. Any spare cash, spend it on a new stadium, or a new pool, or a new dance-floor. Any darn thing, as long as school doesn't get *nasty*."

"Not a bad thing up to a point, surely."

"Sure. But it's got beyond the point. The universities are infected. Apart from the big private places —they're O.K.—college is just a glorified school. Not a place where real intellectual scholars work on a super-adult level, while the youngsters extend their intellects by craning upward. It's the other way round. Our so-called scholars sit and think out smart ways of getting down to the student's level. We ought to toughen up on our kids. Hell, when you come to think of it, they're all this country's got." He looked over at where a bunch of boys and girls were chattering. "Jessie," he said. "Come on here."

Jessie ran up. "Here's a gentleman from England," he said. "Say hullo to him." Jessie said "Hullo." When she went away again, he said: "How old do you think she is?"

I looked after her slim figure, her made-up face, the well-rouged lips and pretty hair. "Sixteen? Sixteen and a half?"

"She's thirteen. She's having a hell of a good time. She oughta be smacked a bit, but it's not allowed. By the way, all these grade schools are going to get psychiatrists permanently on the staff."

"That's very thorough."

"Sure. Childhood in America is a thorough time. A lot of time and money and energy go into it. No wonder we don't want to grow up."

Whether it is due to the co-educational system or to the freedom of the American home, young Americans seem to be much more open about their relations with the opposite sex than they are over here. They begin talking about "dates" and "dating" at an earlier age. Boys visit girls in their own houses, call for them and take them for walks, at an age when in Britain they would still be rendezvousing behind the chapel or in the back row of the cinema. Whereas in Britain many a girl will see a boy a couple of dozen times before she plucks up enough courage to take him home to tea, in America she might try him out on the family the day after she meets him first. The word "Date" itself has a kind of accepted jargonized ring, and even highly educated and sophisticated people use it as good verbal currency. The wife of a university professor will tell you that you have missed seeing her daughter as she is "out on a date." A leader of provincial society might volunteer to you, almost over the teacups, that she doesn't know what will happen, but "Dorothy has been dating steady with John Smith" for nearly six months. Sometimes after a debate there would be a dance nearby. "Would you Oxford gentlemen like to go?" The Oxford gentlemen would. "Shall we fix you up with 'dates'?" You might be standing in a group at a party talking to a young lady. "Oh, by the way," she might say suddenly, pulling on the sleeve of a contiguous male, "I want you to meet my 'date,'" or "You don't say? Well! I must tell that to my 'date.'" Having, or being on, a "date" sounded rather a formal and full-time affair. The young lady would have to be fetched, escorted, protected, and taken home. If a young man "dates" a young lady for a big dance, he must send round a corsage for her. This must match her dress and suit her taste, but he is expected to achieve this without asking her what she wants. "What about a 'date'?" says the boy at a party to a girl who has taken his eye. There is no shy beating about the bush. Both know the minimum that they are in for. Having had one date with each other, neither of them will assume that another need or should follow.

There is a natural connection between dating and the American motor-car. It is comfortable, it is fitted with radio and electric heater, ash-trays, cigarette lighter. It has doors. It is about the only place in America where there is any privacy. The house is a busy thoroughfare; hedges and shady arbours belong to the Old World. It would be unjust to say that the auto has become a substitute for babies. The car is the bridge by which Americans pass from the inhibitions of always living in public to a private life. The Ford V-8 is the American Lovers' Lane, and the crooners deputize for bird-song.

A visitor from Britain would notice one thing about any American home he entered—the comparative simplicity of the family's life. There would be quarrels and snaps, the usual tensions of the blood-relationship and of people living together in a small place, but all much lighter than they seem in Britain. The relationship between American father and son are much more truly brotherly than they are over here. There is none of that unmanning shyness which is papered over here under the "old boy" and "old son" of that pseudo-comradeship to which some Britons are still committed. For his mother, the American boy's feelings are more complicated. The days when an Indian raid could destroy a community's hope of posterity are not so long ago, and the realization of the vulnerability of society through the mother is still vital enough to put an edge on his chivalry towards her. The women, especially the mothers, are more dominating than they are in Britain. Hearing the strength in some of their talking, sensing their independence of the man they have married, you remember that their grandmothers were born with the smell of gunpowder in their nostrils. It is round the mother that the family's feelings centre. It explains why American men, beneath the toughness, can be so tender.

The freeness, the candour, the naturalness of the American home rises out of the way the children are treated—as fully-fledged members of the family. In British families, a visitor is conscious of the "ranks" which still linger: the head of the family, the head of the family's wife, the eldest son, the eldest daughter. Over there, there are two old people and a lot of younger ones. American parents seem to demand much less and expect less than British parents do. They accept the consequences of toleration cheerfully.

One Saturday night, in Melville, I could hear the boy next door arguing with his father. "Why cain't I take it, Dad?" he said once or twice.

"Because it's new, and I don't want it scratched," said his Dad.

"What's going on?" I asked Tom.

"Jim wants to take his father's car down to a dance on the shore," he said, "and his Dad won't let him."

Jim was sixteen. The hour was then eleven o'clock, and the shore was half an hour's drive.

"Well, I don't blame him," I said. "Sixteen years old, driving a car out to a dance at this time."

"Oh, that ain't what his paw's grousing about," said Tom. "He don't mind the kid goin' in his *own* car. It's lending him his that he don't want."

"Well," I said, "you may think I sound a prig——"

"What's that?"

I explained.

"We don't have 'em here. But g'wan."

"I may sound a heel," I said, "but I think that kind of freedom's going too far."

"Well, I guess you're right maybe. But we let the kids get on with it. See, we don't figure it's logical to wrap 'em up in cotton-wool at seventeen, and send 'em out to bomb Berlin a few months later. But maybe you're right."

For me, it was a memorable experience to spend Christmas in an American home. It was moving to see how Christmas brought out the brightest and the warmest in both peoples. In America, it was a time of Christmas trees and never-ending carols. Every house seemed to have its little tree, in the front window or on the porch, glittering with hoar-frost and glowing with coloured lights. Inside the houses were evergreens and flowers rather than lanterns and streamers. Carols poured around us from radio, gramophone and the piano next door. Easily the favourite was "Silent Night." Served up in different rhythms or settings it never seemed to stop. At midnight on Christmas Eve it came over the air on fifteen different stations at once. On Christmas Day everybody gave everybody presents. Even though you were an unexpected last-minute visitor, rather than see you without a gift, they'd surreptitiously snap off their watch-chain and give it you in a hastily-wrapped piece of tissue-paper. As with us, the informing spirit of their Christmas, after Christ's, is that of Dickens. Scrooge comes hardy and annual over the Christmas radio air. America's Christmas is as good—and as old—as ours.

CHAPTER IX

American Law and Order

THE quickest guide to a country's kind of law and order is a glance at its policemen. The slow, steady gait of the British bobby is the pace of an old and law-abiding country. It belongs to the village green, to Parliament Square, to the solid, profitable interest which a nation of shopkeepers had in the king's peace.

The first American policeman I saw was on the outskirts of New York. He was standing on the centre of a crossing directing the traffic. In his mouth was a whistle which he blew almost continuously. He signalled vigorously with both arms. Sometimes his gestures said things which were not polite. Occasionally he took the whistle from his mouth to shout at someone who was driving too fast, or at someone who was driving too slow. Once he stopped all the traffic to let some children cross the road. He took the two smallest by the hand and, as they toddled along with him, he asked the bigger ones how they liked the new schoolteacher. Five minutes later he had ordered a large coach to pull in to the kerb: it had missed a signal. He stalked over to it, and began to berate the driver. "If you think you can drive like that in *my* street . . ." he said several times. The driver drooped miserably out of the window. The policeman would go back, direct more traffic, and stalk over to the coach again. "If you think you can do that to me, brother . . ." His tough, good-natured Irish face was plum-coloured with personal, rather than official, indignation.

The people in New York tell you they have need of their police. "Be careful of your bill-fold—I mean your wallet," they would say. The second day of our stay there we went into a big bank to cash a cheque. It was many flights up; you climbed the first twenty floors by express lift, then you changed to a slow, stopping one. All the cashiers worked behind heavy grills. We collected our notes, and took them to a table so that we could share them out. "You boys cain't do that here," said a friendly voice. It was one of the fully-armed, top-booted policemen who walked on every floor. "And don't flash any bills in the street," he called, as we re-entered the lift. "People round here'll do anything for money."

Not that New Yorkers cannot look after themselves. That night Edward and I ate supper in what, in London, would have been a Lyons' Corner House. Everybody sat and ate with their hats on. Half-way through my meal there was a rustle behind us. Looking around we saw a middle-aged man, smoothly and scientifically propelling a ragged tough towards the door. He came back in, readjusted his tie, and chatted casually with the girl at the pay-desk. It was all, apparently, in the day's work. Apart from us nobody had stopped eating.

Two days later I was travelling on the train from Jersey City to Newark. I wanted to pass from one coach to another, but three or four people were blocking the way. Peeping between their shoulders, I could see two little men, at the end of the second coach, aiming wild blows at each other. Both were in their stockinged feet. After a few more lunges the bigger of the two withdrew into our coach. The smaller one threw his shoes after him, and then sat down. Our little group pursued its way into the coach without comment. Nobody seemed to notice anything odd. Most people continued to read newspapers, though a woman with a shopping-basket complained that people oughtn't to "get in the way," and a man wearing a tie with a dancing-girl worked on it shook the little man by the hand and said: "You're a real man. The lug had it coming."

A month later we were a thousand miles away. Chokeynne was one of the few big towns of a wide mining and timber district. It stood amongst forest, falls and mountain valleys. The Professor of Speech told us that we were very fortunate: Mr. Gordon, one of the wealthiest men in the district, had offered to put us up for the week-end. "He's got a lovely house," said the Professor. "Some say the best in the whole state."

It was a lovely house. The library was the best private collection I saw in the States, and the wall of every room —again no doors—was hung with paintings by modern French and British masters. Each had its own concealed lighting. In the dining-room was a small Goya. Mr. Gordon, white-haired, scholarly and kind, showed us round. "By the way," he said, "be careful of the guns."

"Guns?"

"Yes. They're all over the place. Loaded."

"Really."

"Pretty tough country hereabouts," he said. "Now and again somebody takes a dislike to you. And there's a lot of valuable stuff in the house. Cousin of mine got kidnapped couple of years ago. No good relying on the police."

"Aren't they good round here?"

"They're fine, but they're a long way off. What's the use of good police miles away when somebody's coming in through the window? That's why there's a gun in every room. Might as well put up a fight."

That afternoon we all went down into the cellar. Even quite small American houses seem to have a cellar. Many families fit them up as bars or "Rumpus Rooms" where they or the children can have a good party without untidying the rest of the house. Mr. Gordon's cellar was fitted up as a thirty-foot, miniature rifle-range. In the racks were a couple of twelve-bores, an eighteen-bore, a twenty-bore, an automatic rifle and a couple of .303's. Mr. Gordon picked one up.

"Fine job, these," he said reflectively.

"What d'you use them for?"

"Oh, anything that comes along. Had one out the other day. They don't often go on strike around here, but when they do, they don't like seeing anybody else on the job. My boys were taking some stuff across the river; they were a bit scared that some roughs were going to stop 'em. So I went out midstream in a rowboat with this." He lay down on the firing-mat, pushed his thick-lensed spectacles up on to his benign brow, and began to shoot. His first five shots cut the middle out of the target.

One of the pistols he showed me was a funny little thing which had two barrels, separate trigger, no chamber, and broke at the butt. "Gambler's pistol," he said. "Only two shots. Just enough to get the light out and drop the guy who was after you. Not bulky. Fits in your sleeve, like this." He demonstrated.

"It looks quite up to date," I said.

"It is. Old folks round here have seen 'em used."

That night my bedroom was the loveliest room I had ever slept in. On the wall were three charming little eighteenth-century French landscapes, with shepherdesses, wispy trees and aristocratic-looking sheep. An elegant chandelier hung down from the centre of the ceiling. By the bedside stood a small Sheraton table. I pulled open its drawer. There lay a Colt .38, the rims of the brass shells grinning through the lips of the cylinder. "Art gallery or arsenal?" I wondered, as I fell asleep.

Our visit to Lyonsville fell on the day of a big football

match. We arrived about five o'clock. Within a few minutes the newsboys were running all over the town, their headlines crying "Student Visitor Shot." Hastily the Oxford debaters counted themselves. They were all there.

Next day the story appeared. After celebrating the result of the football match, one of the students was walking a little unsteadily along a narrow street in the French Quarter. Around a sharp corner came a motorist. The student was nearly knocked down. "——!" he called out to the disappearing car. The car stopped. The driver got out and walked back. "Call me that again," he said. "——!" said the student. Next moment he was on the ground with a bullet in him. The motorist drove off.

What interested us most about this incident was the attitude of the inhabitants towards it. It would be unjust to suggest that, judging by papers and conversation, this kind of thing seemed to go on every day. But there was no mistaking their accepting that . . . well, this kind of thing did happen. Like travelling, they took violent crime in their stride. There was something casual in the way they spoke of it.

There was something casual even in the way they acted. A fortnight later, whilst my friends were finishing their tea, I was standing at the desk of a small southern state hotel, waiting for our bill. Suddenly, as I leaned on the counter, reading my paper, I became aware that there was a big, heavily-built, untidy man also leaning on the counter a few feet away. The young lady who was making out the bill cast occasional glances at him. There was something odd about him; whether he was drunk, mentally deranged, or very fatigued I could not say but, whatever it was, I hoped I would not have to find out. As I was being handed my change the door opened.

Two policemen stepped in. They had quietly crossed the room, run their hands over the big man's belt and pockets for a gun, and whisked him out before my change was in my pocket. Yet there seemed no hurry. The cashier went on with her figures, and a man reading his paper on the settee merely looked over the top. In these circumstances I felt it would have shown a morbid curiosity to ask what exactly was going on.

A people's sense of law and order comes out in the way they behave when they are not being supervised. The British are, for instance, good queuers—because they have learned that sometimes it pays to get in line. The Americans not only hate queueing; they do not know how to do it. At bus stations or railways there are sometimes chains or barriers which pen them into some sort of line. Otherwise they stand around a bus-stop or railway train door in a big bunch. If it is a rush hour, they surge forward and jostle vigorously for position. You get no credit for giving up your place: unless you had been standing in one of these fenced-in lanes you never had a place. It is not so much "first come, first served," as "first to get it, first served."

This national dislike and incapacity for "getting into line" comes out in the way they drive their motor-cars. It is a convention that when two cars are approaching each other they should both keep to their right-hand side. Apart from that, the road is free, and the American passes, holds the centre, nips in and out of the line, and roars along two and three abreast till he or one of his companions gives way.

Much national character lies behind the way the Britisher and the American uses the "bumpers" on the front of their motor-cars. For the Britisher they are there for emergency: if he is bumped into by another car, the bumpers will protect his paintwork. The American, on the other hand, uses his "fenders" to "fend off" other cars which might happen to get in his way. He will back his car into a wall, not until he feels he is nearly touching it, but until his "fenders" give it a good smack. Then he will drive forward confidently till he has given a good tap to the car in front. He will use them, like antennæ or cats' whiskers, to feel his way in and out of a parking jam, and to find a pair of "fenders" still looking bright new is naturally rare.

The manners of both peoples have something in common with the way they use their bumpers.

American drivers drive much faster than British, and with far more initiative and self-confidence. They will often get into a block at a crossing or a defile, but they never need a policeman to get them out. They shout at each other, perhaps, and honk loudly on their hooters, but their minds—and their accelerators—work swiftly, and the road is cleared in no time. Americans drive much more boldly than the British—they seem not to be inhibited by the thought of an accident, nor the thought of going to court. They do not want a "ticket," but only because it means a fine, not because it involves an appearance in court, before the symbolized majesty of law and order. Law and order, government, to the American, is never awesome. It is not a dread and dominating father who looks sternly down and evokes in the subject a not wholly rational sense of guilt. It is just a big brother—sometimes an interfering nuisance, as big brothers often are. But a nuisance who, on the whole, means well, whose ankle can be kicked, whose shirts can be pinched, and who will, now and then, stump up a birthday present if you treat him properly.

You feel this strongly when you talk to an American policeman. He may be pleasant, unpleasant, friendly or unfriendly, rude or courteous, call you "Sir" or "Bud," depending on whether he is busy or at leisure, an anti-British ex-Dubliner, a part-time university student, or a waggish ex-bootlegger. Whatever he is, he will be an individual. He will not, in his bearing nor even in his voice, suggest the distant, but informing, majesty and solemnity of the British Law as even the village policeman does—"Hi called upon haccused to desist, whereupon 'e responded . . ." The American policeman knows that he is on the job to stop trouble of any sort, and more often than not he has been given a gun. He thinks more about keeping order than of representing an historic law. He may be a pillar of society, but he talks and walks like an American dressed up in uniform.

The inherited feeling of protection, on the physical level, which the Englishman has, may make him seem a little timid, or fussy, to some Americans. After our visit to the Grand Canyon we were being driven across the flat scant pasture of Nevada to the nearest airport. Our driver was a cowboyish-looking fellow with one of those big grey felt hats which they measure by the gallon. He had been a cattle-man, until a film company came to make a film in the district. Then he made a living falling off horses in films where the silver-spurred, white-horsed hero was firing from the saddle, and bringing down the leaders of the pursuing Indian host.

"It must have been painful," I said.

"You get the knack of it purty soon. You let yourself go limp."

"Didn't you ever get hurt?"

"Only once. Was lying on the ground, resting, and the camera-wagon rode over me. Said they thought I was a dummy."

I looked out of the window. All around was flat until, on the horizon, the hills of the San José mountains suddenly shot up into the duck-egg blue of the sky, as though somebody had sketched them as a mural. "What's law and order like round here?" I said.

"O.K."

"You look a bit like cowboys I've seen on the films." (Though he was driving what might have been a 1950 version of the big Humber shooting-brake.) "Is it like the films at all here now?"

"No. Things is pretty quiet now."

"Do you still have the sheriff with his star?"

"Oh, sure."

"Is he elected?"

"Sure. We got our noo one last week."

"What happens to the old one?"

"Nothing. He died."

"What happened to him?"

"He got shot up."

"H'm. You said things weren't like the films!"

"Sure. Don't pay any attention to 'em. You see guys firing maybe twelve shots out of a six-gun without loading. Cain't be done. Tain't right thet kind of lies go career'n' round the world. And you see a guy rid'n' a pony down a cliff so steep, th' hocks is grind'n' on the stones. A horseman wouldn't use a pony like that. No wonder other folks thinks bad of us Americans. No wonder they think we're rough."

As we bumped and bounded on the long, straight, but not even road I thought about the places I had seen along the rim of the Grand Canyon where a grown-up could have slipped, or leaped, to a five-thousand-foot death. Then I thought of where a single iron spar stands between the onlooker and the torrent at Niagara, that pours over the precipice two yards or so from his feet. Railways without fences, motors parked in the high street without lights, traffic signals without the amber warning, and a hundred other situations where the Englishman would be roping off, or putting up notices of "Danger: Beware!"

"Many people fall down the Canyon?" I asked.

"Sure."

"I'm not surprised. I saw a dozen places on the rim where I had to walk very carefully."

"Sure."

"I think those places ought to be fenced off."

"Why?"

"Well, they're so damn' dangerous."

"You get giddy or sum'pn'?"

"It's not a question of getting giddy or anything. It's simply that people, especially children, might fall over. As, indeed, you say they do."

"You cain't do people's living for 'em, brother. Besides, how in tarnation you goin' to fence in the whole of the canyon? There ain't that much fence in the whole of the state. If you wanna go up there and have a peek, you've gotta watch out for yourself."

American society still expects the individual to watch out for himself. He seems, so far, to like it that way.

CHAPTER X

Americans and their Politics

ALIGHTING from the Pullman car on which we had spent the last eighteen hours, we looked at the grim, dirty, bepuddled New Orleans railway station.

"Pardon me, are you the gen'l'men from Oxford . . .?"

In a few minutes we were sitting with two boys from the university eating breakfast in one of New Orleans' best hotels.

"You English?" asked the waitress.

"Yes."

"Come from London?" Americans think that nearly everybody in Britain lives in London.

"No. But my friend here lives there some of the year."

"Where do you live?"

"I live in Wiltshire."

"My husband was over there in the war. He was in a place called Devonshire." She made shire rhyme with fire. "Is that anywheres near Wiltshire?"

"Well, there's about forty miles between their nearest points."

"Now is that all?" Obviously, she was about to ask if I bumped into him, but changed her mind. "I'd have the liver," she advised cordially. "It's real good this morning." She went off. For the rest of the meal I could see her having hasty, whispered conversations with other waitresses, turning her eyes—and theirs—in our direction. She was telling them that her husband and I had been next door to one another.

"We've looked forward to coming to New Orleans," I said to Jim Bone, our host.

"You've heard about the French Quarter?"

"Not because of that. I'm told that most Europeans find it disappointing, anyway."

"Food?"

"No."

"What then?"

"Well, I've read so much and heard so much about Huey Long, I've wanted to see the place he lived in."

"Uh-huh."

"He did a lot of good for this state," said the other boy.

"Tom means he gave the people a lot of things they wanted," said Bob. "Parks, schools, hospitals. But all pushed through any way he could push them through. The government of this state was just one big racket."

"Bob's a bit prejudiced," said Jim.

"Maybe I am a bit prejudiced," said Bob. "My father lost his job because he wouldn't play ball with the Long outfit."

"I'm sorry," I said. "Was he a politician? Or a government official?"

"Official nothing. He was just a professor at the university."

"Good God!"

"What's the matter? Don't you get political graft in universities in Britain?"

"Well . . . er . . . I really don't know, Bob. But I don't think we get that kind of thing."

"Never?"

"Well, er . . . It may happen sometimes, but there'd be an awful song and dance if they found it out. It certainly can't happen nearly as much over there as with you."

"How do you know?"

"If it did, I wouldn't exclaim 'Good God!' when I heard of an example. I'd talk about it as casually as you do."

Next morning, Bob and Tom took us out to Baton Rouge to see the State Capitol which Huey Long had built. We saw the great, much-terraced building rising grandly from artful vistas and well-regimented lawns, the tall clay-coloured tower soaring above the olive greens and duns of the shabby sub-tropical landscape. We saw the two great council chambers where each handsome desk was equipped with a microphone, the great ornamented doors, and the corridor where the assassin's bullet brought down the unsuspecting governor, and where the blast from the machine-guns of his guards chipped star-shaped scars upon the marble walls. From the tower we gazed down on the swards and trim box hedges, upon a hospital he had built, upon his statue and memorial in the heart of the pleasant gardens.

"How tragic," I said, "that good men can do bad things."

"The real tragedy for us," said Bob, "is that bad men can do good things."

Politics in the United States tend to be cruder than in Britain. The man in the street frankly regards politics as a pretty dirty business. We passed through one state capital a few days before the election of the state governor. In the evening edition of the leading paper there were letters from the two main candidates. Candidate Smith told the electors that Candidate Brown had been a grafter, an embezzler, a liar, a briber and a corrupter and, into the bargain, had betrayed his own (Brown's) brother. (Brown's brother had been a very popular governor of that state.) Candidate Brown was just as eloquent about Smith. In Smith's previous tenure of office, he said, he had not only practically ruined the state in a general kind of way, but he had also diverted public moneys into the party chest and into his own pocket. The vigour, frankness and thoroughness with which each informed the electors of the other's unfitness to serve them, was something I would not have believed if I had not read it. Had anything like *either* charge-sheet appeared in Britain, the victim would have been in honour bound to have attacked it in the courts. If by some chance *two* such charge-sheets appeared in the same election, British public life would have collapsed. Indeed, only when British public conscience *had* disappeared could the occasion have arisen for such mutual mud-slinging.

When we were in his home State of Missouri, we were asked what the British thought of Mr. Truman.

"Considering he took over from such a great man, and hadn't been heard of before, they think pretty well of him."

"I wish we could."

"Well, that's your business. And I suppose you know the facts. As far as we're concerned, he's a decent chap, and the leader of the party."

"The guy's a heel," broke in another lad. "He was one of the biggest grafters in Kansas. And boy! was there competition in Kansas! Ever hear of Prendergast?"

"Vaguely."

"Prendergast was a gambler. Horses, business, any darn thing. He used bribes, forged election lists, phoney voters, the whole darn shooting-match to keep control of that state. Even force. And Truman started in politics as one of his gang."

"Now look here, Leo," said one of his friends, "you cain't prove that."

"Has Truman ever denied he worked for Prendergast?"

"No. He hasn't."

"All right. Didn't he go to Tom Prendergast's funeral?"

"Yes, he did."

"And didn't he do that when his own friends advised him not to 'cos it would look bad? Answer me that, now."

"He admits he became Senator because of Prendergast, but he always swears that, not only did he not *do* anything wrong, but that Prendergast never asked him to. And he said that Prendergast was a good and honest friend to him, and that he owed it to his memory to walk behind the hearse. Nobody c'n deny it. So in that case, ain't it good, not bad, to go to the funeral?"

"Waal. What do you say, Ken?"

"I don't know what the facts are. But I think people don't mind a man who's been wrong, as long as it's not too wrong, if he's got the guts to admit it."

"Sure. But now I do grant this against Truman. He may be honest, I think he is. But he's no business man. No, sir, that he is not. Do you know, after the last war, he set up a haberdashery store. And the darn thing went bust! That alone might have lost him a coupla million votes."

"But, good Lord! A good President needn't be a good haberdasher."

"It don't do for him to be a bad one. Lots of Americans don't feel like trusting men who go into business and lose money. We don't mind 'em losing other people's, mind, or losing public money. But when they fool about and lose their own—well, they've had it. Which is one reason why I used to think Mr. Martin might become President. He not only started from the bottom without a penny, he started on money he borrowed!"

Quite separate from the cynicism with which many Americans look at politics and public life, is the egalitarian passion many of them have for abusing and ridiculing those in authority. It is the former that makes many say that F. D. Roosevelt was a crook; it is the latter that causes them to say what is almost the opposite: that he went into politics because he was not smart enough for business. The average American does not believe that politics and affairs *are* in the hands of business men: what he believes is that it would be all right if they *were*.

This irreverent attitude to great national figures is peculiarly American. It expresses itself in various ways. Mrs. Roosevelt's personality and appearance is a stock subject for coarse humour. In the radio shows of the Bob Hope and Jack Benny type there are plenty of cracks about "Harry," and when Miss Margaret Truman made her debut as a singer, America's comedians made millions rock with laughter which was not always kindly.

Especially when discussing foreign potentates and royalty, one senses a feeling of romantic envy, possibly of historical inferiority, behind the cutting-edge of American sarcasm. Jokes about American heiresses, daughters of meat-packers and corn-cob kings who have come back from Europe with a medieval coat-of-arms in their buttonhole, are traditional. Movie news shots of European royalty are a blend of childish reverence and of almost sadistic candour, a sequence of stately and panoplied shots of crownings and accolades, followed by a glimpse of an inebriated royal yawn, or the sound of a regal stammer. Foreign princelings are spoken and written of with a sometimes good-humoured contempt, and egalitarian intimacy, which few writers would dream of using in discussing the Hollywood film stars. The latter belong utterly to the world of romance. Only the flesh and the blood is heir to the ills of American wisecrack.

There is something odd about the way the American

will not stand for the petty follies of plush and velvet, the golden swords and black silk knee-breeches at St. James's, and the flowing scarlet of our Doctors of Divinity, and yet will tolerate the far more harmful and less decorative follies of her public men. It is as though decadence is only recognized when it is adorning; the tough kind is allowed to get away with it. One night, at a debate in New England, one of the debaters said in our debate on Nationalization that the idea of putting industry into the hands of politicians was insane. "I suppose," he said into the microphone which bore his words not only into the Speech Library of records, but out into the local city, "we shall have the local railways run by people like Hiram Furloe." There was a loud laugh. I gathered from a few statements made by the speaker that Mr. Furloe was the local mayor, and that the speaker thought he ought to be in gaol. After the debate I talked to him about it.

"That was a bit steep, Jim," I said. "Lugging in the mayor like that."

"He's a regular heel, Ken," he said. "Nothing's too bad for him."

"But couldn't he come back at you for saying so over the air? Anywhere in public, for that matter?"

"What for?"

"For saying you think he should be in gaol."

"But so he should, Kennie. Most everybody round here thinks so too. There was a lot of protest about the pardon."

"About the what?"

"The pardon. They let him out before his time was up."

"From gaol?"

"Sure."

"And he's back in office?"

"Sure."

"What was he in gaol *for*?"

"I think it was for stealing some of the registered mail. Or was that the last time? Either stealing registered mail, or taking some public money. Something like that."

"Well!"

"Don't you get heels like that sometimes?"

"Yes, I suppose we do. But not often. And even if a British mayor did go to gaol, even if, perhaps, a British mayor went to gaol *twice*, I don't think he'd be allowed to go on mayoring."

"That's just our belief in human nature, Kennie. Lots of us don't want to support the unemployed, because we believe God helps only those who help themselves. But we're ready to give the mayor a second chance, bless him."

When things like this happen, it is easy to understand why, sometimes, the attitude of America's leading magazines towards politicians is cynical and bitter almost to the point of masochism. Recently in one of them there was a photograph of a mayor holding a little girl. Sitting on his office sofa was the little girl's mother, and her two other children. She had come along to the mayor, said the magazine, to ask if, somewhere in the overcrowded district, he could find her somewhere to live. The mayor found a place. Then, according to the magazine report, he had that photograph taken and circulated in order to impress his electorate with his zeal on their behalf. The caption beneath the photograph went on to add, amongst other gratuitous information touching on the mayor's motives in performing this apparent act of public spirit, that he had recently been in gaol.

If an Englishman were asked by a visiting American to explain the Party system, he would probably do so in terms of the party programme or, if he wanted to discuss their differences on an ideological plane, in terms of the historical principles for which they had given battle. If an American were doing the same job for a visiting Englishman, he would probably talk in terms of "pressure groups." The American political party is an alliance of sections representing different interests, such as business, financial, labour, agricultural, which go to make up the texture of the national, economic and social life. On the whole, these elements have allied themselves round the Democrat or Republican banner in terms of local politics and issues. Labour, therefore, might be Republican in one state and Democrat in another. Local labour, having done its bit to get, say, the Democrat in charge of the machine of national administration, hopes that whenever the machine bears on their local affairs, it will bear in the way they want. Trade relations, government contracts, offices and local regulations are distributed by those in power. They are the fruits for which the electors have laboured.

In a big country, it is these local interests rather than the national affairs which, in the past, have loomed in the citizen's mind. For him the "common good" has not meant so much the United States as his own state. As there may often be a cleavage between the good of his own state, and the good of the States as a whole, he is not as keen to talk about the national good as perhaps the Britisher is. And since he knows that the national good in such a vast and differing land as the United States cannot be the same everywhere, he knows that somebody is going to be disappointed, and somebody is going to be pleased at nearly every decision which is taken at Washington. The "national good" is not something which grows on a tree, to be sought if the harvester will only look hard enough for it. It is something that emerges from a pretty fierce argument, and however good it is, somebody is going to find it bad. He hopes, and tries hard to ensure, that it won't be him. He won't squeal if it is. He won't listen to those who do, if it isn't.

Being accustomed to this kind of "pressure" politics, Americans are less squeamish than other nations about the relations between political and non-political concerns. "There's only one thing wrong with the president of our university," said one student to me. "He's a Republican."

"Well, that's all right, surely."

"Yes. But if he were a Democrat, he'd be able to do more good in this state."

"But surely, if he's an able man, the state will want him to do all the good he can whatever his political views."

"Yes. But the Democrats run things here, and you can't expect them to give posts to any person who won't vote for them."

"Why should he vote for them if he doesn't trust them?"

"Why should they trust him if he don't trust *them*? And why should they give big educational posts to Republicans when there's plenty of Democrats around?"

"But he might be better than any of the Democrats."

"In a big country like this, when you can't always be keeping an eye on what goes on, you can't rely on just 'good' men. You've got to have them bound to you, running in the same harness. Better off with loyal guys who aren't so hot than with smart ones you can't count on."

Another effect of the size of the country, of the difficulty in uniting scattered outposts and reconciling different interests, is the premium set on strong men and colourful personalities. This is one of the explanations of the careers of men like Huey Long, and the reason why the local or party "boss" is such an important figure in

American politics. Colourful personality is sometimes just as valuable and efficient as strength. In some places the kind of clown governor, who marks his appearance in town by kissing all the women in sight, and then curling up for a nap on the pavement of the High Street, is more effective than a rich or a learned man. Publicity, photographs in the paper, rumours, appearances with distinguished visitors, inaugurating exhibitions and attending ball-games—they are all part of the great semaphore whereby the face of government is relayed all over the State, as the Indian once sent his smoke. Greatest of all uniting forces, and the newest handmaiden of government is the radio. A good voice, and a good manner on the air, maybe, is the most important asset of a candidate for a big election. The voice of F. D. Roosevelt was the silver thread which wove more unity into the United States than they had ever known.

One day, whilst people in New York were digging themselves out of a million snowdrifts, I lay on the edge of a swimming-pool in Florida. Dark green, flimsy Spanish moss hung, like a girl's green hair, upon the southern trees. A student called Fritz Meyer was stretched upon the bank, whilst his sister swam, smoothly and silently, in the water, her brown back glistening in America's most expensive sun. I looked at the list of candidates for the Presidential election.

"Looks as if Eisenhower won't run."

"Good thing," said Fritz.

"I'm surprised to hear that. He's clearly a fine fellow, and he's almost as respected abroad as he is in America."

"Sure."

"Well, what's wrong with him?"

"He's a soldier."

"What's wrong with soldiers?"

"Nothing. It's just a pity that we have to turn to

military men so often in our history for leadership. It's not healthy."

"I don't see that it matters. If the soldier doesn't try to run the government as he used to run his troops, there's no harm in it, is there?"

"There's a risk," said Fritz. "Our political life doesn't produce as many purely civil great men as our government could use. Military figures have a great and glorious tradition in our history. When a big, wide, far-flung country like ours has to be unified, very often only the great military autocrats can do it. The pomp, and the glamour, and the martial law work where a freer and slower, more local, authority doesn't."

"Well, that's all very well," I said. "But good Americans, as far as I can see, don't want to be all that unified. And they're not that keen on efficient and speedy government. They'd prefer to be far-flung, inefficient, slow and free."

"Yes. But only as long as they feel they're secure, politically and economically. If there's a great threat from outside, and if we suddenly feel our bread and butter endangered inside, we might want to get together quick."

"So what?"

"So our military men would get to work on our military streak——"

"Gosh, Fritz. D'you really think that America has a military streak? When you wear those floppy blouses, and the men hardly ever bother to salute?"

"Of course we have a military streak. Haven't you seen our bands at football matches, the Stars and Stripes at the debates, that kind of hysterical bloodlust we work up for big ball-games, and the way we let our police force punch us around? Boy, we ache for a fight, and we love that martial music."

"My dear Fritz," I said. "When the Senate Committee has just finished a probe into Communist activities, are you trying to say that America might go Fascist?"

"Those names, those labels, mean nothing to me," he said. "All I know is that the people of this country may one day wake up with a bump and find their political system isn't good enough for them. They'll be so keen to get rid of graft and inefficiency maybe they'll go too far and too quick. We Americans are like that, sometimes. We're not good at getting round to things slowly. We like to have a sudden drive. And sometimes we drive right into trouble."

CHAPTER XI

Americans Keep One Guessing

"SPEED, enterprise, zipp," said the colonel. He and I stood in the village street in 1942. "That's what I used to think of Americans," he added. "Well, look at those." He pointed to where three American soldiers strolled along in the sun, their hands in their pockets, their caps tilted back on their heads. "Lounging," said the colonel. "You'd think they didn't know what hurry was." At that moment a jeep shot around the corner at such a speed that the colonel's hat blew off. "Good God!" he said. "The way these chaps drive! It's a public menace."

It is difficult to generalize about the Americans: as a people they seem to show a number of qualities which are contradictory.

Of all the contradictions the one most likely to strike a foreigner is the way they take some things more seriously than we do, and other things more lightly.

Before we could disembark at New York, we had to show our Immigration Officer a certificate to prove we had been vaccinated within the last two years. As we stood in the long queue waiting our turn with the Immigration Officer, I saw that a number of people were being turned back. As they passed us their faces wore expressions of bewilderment. I stopped one of them. "What's going on up there?" I said.

"I've got to go and be vaccinated by the ship's M.O."

"What for?"

"My vaccination certificate doesn't say that I had a positive reaction."

"What's a positive reaction?"

"A blister."

"But mine doesn't say I had a blister."

"You might as well come and be done too."

"But wait a minute," I said. "Even if you get vaccinated again now, you won't be able to raise a blister right away. Will you have to stay on the ship till it comes up?"

"No," he said. "But if the ship's M.O. does it they'll feel you've been done properly."

"What it comes to then," I said, "is that unless your certificate says you've had a blister, they assume your doctor didn't do the job. But if the ship's M.O. does you, they assume that you'll get a blister."

"That's right," he said. He moved off, feeling for the two dollars which was the ship's vaccination fee.

In front of me was a big American wearing a white panama. He turned around to me. "You can't afford dollars for this kind of nonsense," he said. "You just do what I do."

I studied him carefully. When the official took my certificate, and asked, "Have you a positive reaction?" I said: "Yes."

"It doesn't say so on your certificate."

"The chap who did me didn't know it had to say it."

"Describe the reaction."

"First it got sore, then it blistered, then there was some pus, then it went."

I got through. As the American in the white panama said afterwards, there was no need to say that the positive reaction took place seven years ago. I wasn't asked about that.

"From what I'd heard about the Americans," I said, "I'd have thought they'd be the last people to fuss about things like that."

"You'll find a lot of that in the States," he said. "See, son, as a people we haven't got what you might call 'regulation sense.' We follow rules literally, well, because we're afraid that if we don't we might get the wool pulled over us. We haven't developed official discretion—we're either very slack or very pedantic about them. I guess particularly when there's foreigners around we try and impress them that we aren't the easy-going folks we might be taken for."

At one of the New York railway stations, Edward and I went to the baggage-room where we had deposited our suit-cases. Edward found that he had mislaid his ticket. I looked across the long low steel-topped counter at the little man in charge.

"My friend here," I said, displaying the other tickets, "has lost his check. I am afraid our train leaves in fifteen minutes."

"No check, no baggage," said the little man. "Regulations."

"I think you might be able to identify us," I said. "We only put them in last night. Perhaps you remember our English clothes?"

The little man screwed up his face in an effort of recollection. "Three grips?"

"That's right. About six p.m."

He thought for a few moments. "Sure," he said, with a touch of pride in his voice. "Sure, sure. Three grips. Two brown, one blue, huh?"

"That's absolutely right. Good show. It's that blue one we want."

"No check, no baggage," he said. "Regulations, bud."

This was the last occasion on which we lost a baggage check.

We could not foresee all the occasions on which regulations would loom upon us. A fortnight later as we stood with our Canadian friends watching the Niagara pour over into the huge foaming pool, somebody said: "Let's take them over to see what it's like from the States' side." We walked over the long, slender span which carries the road across the Niagara river from the Canadian to the American side. When we came to the U.S. frontier guards, who stood at a kind of turnstile entrance with pistols at their belts, the Canadians walked through unchallenged, Edward and I among them.

Anthony had been walking a few yards behind on his own. The guards accosted him. "Where do you come from?" we heard them ask.

"London," said Anthony truthfully, though not unaware that there is a London not far from Niagara.

"Which London?"

"London, England."

"Passport, please."

Anthony had left it locked in his brief-case in the motor-car. The fact that this was the famous unarmed frontier, and that there were six Canadians and two British citizens who could vouch for Anthony seemed not to matter. We had to watch him deport himself back to the Canadian side.

When we visited West Point, the most famous of all America's great military academies, we were welcomed by some young cadets and two regular army colonels. We were struck by the friendly and informal relations between the cadets and their distinguished superiors. As we walked around the beautiful grounds on the banks of the Hudson we chatted about discipline. One of the colonels told us some of the stories the British soldiers told about American discipline. The best was the story about the American general's conference on discipline with the British Chief-of-Staff.

"Waal," says the American general, "I guess having only just got mobilized our discipline needs tightening. But, mark you, since the boys have been over here with you British their discipline's tightened up a whole lot."

At that moment the door opens and the American general's driver pops his head round. "Say, General," he said. "Is it O.K. if I take your auto to-night? I wanna go dancing."

"Sure," says the general. "Now get outah here—I'm busy."

The door closes. "There now, you see what I mean," he says to the British Chief-of-Staff. "Before that guy came over here, he'd have taken that car without bothering to tell me."

While we were still laughing at this, a bell rang. From all sides cadets poured out of the rooms on their way to their next classes. We noticed that some of the boys walked very elaborately "at attention." Their backs were like pokers, and their chins were rammed back into their high tight collars.

"First year men," said the colonel. "They have to walk everywhere like that."

That night we dined in the great hall. Three of these juniors sat at our table. They were not allowed to talk, and they were not allowed to bend, or to look to right or left. Their chins were still crushed back into their throats. They could hardly swallow.

"I can understand you wanting to discipline them," said Anthony, who, we found later, had collected a long list of "disciplinary" features. "But where's the point in making them eat with their chins pulled in?"

"Discipline," said the colonel. "We believe in making these boys learn to do things just because they're told to."

At the West Point debate we had the biggest audience we ever struck. Every cadet in the place turned up, except the sentries. We felt very flattered till we heard that attendance was compulsory.

Next day we visited Grandtown. The visit was typical of many others. The Professor of Speech and the president of the Student's Union met us off the train. By the time we had covered the five-mile motor trip to the university we all knew each other's Christian names and were conversing like old friends. We lunched informally in the cafeteria, and students came up and greeted us. To other members of the staff we were given brief, off-hand, but friendly introductions. After lunch we went to see the president of the university. In his comfortable armchairs, we lounged back and smoked his cigarettes. He chaffed the students who were with us —he seemed to know them all personally—and told us of how he was arrested in mistake for another president of the same name who had been trying to flee to Canada with the university scholarship funds.

"Right," he said, as we left. "I'll be seeing all you boys to-night."

When we got to the debate hall we found that on the stage, in addition to the chairs for the debaters, there were five other seats. When the curtain was drawn back and the audience became visible, the president advanced to the rostrum. He made a short speech and introduced the Professor of International Affairs. The latter made a short speech and introduced the president of the Union. The president introduced the British Vice-Consul, who made a very short speech, and handed over to the Professor of Speech. The Professor of Speech introduced the Oxford debaters. He went into great detail about our ages, our names, our subjects, our war careers, what we had done at Oxford, and with what political parties our views were associated. Like many other Professors of Speech, in his effort to omit none of the formalities, he got a bit muddled in his notes. This occasion was outstanding. Anthony was described as Sir Wedgewood Binn, a Socialist M.P., and myself as David K. Paris, founder of the Oxford *Isis*. Edward, who became confused with his father, was announced as Chairman of the Balkan Commission in 1924, when Edward was two years old.

After the debate there was a reception in the big dining-room behind the debate hall. The Oxford debaters, the president, the Professor of Speech, and the American debaters were picketed at the door. All the guests filed by each one of us, shaking hands. The president, who was up forward, introduced the first guest to the Professor of Speech. The professor introduced the guest to the first American debater. And so on. It was a considerable piece of drill. As we knew most of the guests already, we felt a little foolish.

The refreshments were laid out on a handsome oval table. At one end, behind a big silver tea urn, sat a lady looking very much gowned. At the other end, also delightfully dressed, but behind a big silver coffee urn, sat another lady. Both wore hats. When the door duty was over, the Oxford men were led over to the table for refreshments. But before they were asked whether they would take tea or coffee, they were introduced to the two presiding ladies. The cups were of fine china, and the cutlery was silver. All the guests were given small, elegantly-worked lace napkins. Everything was very swish. What with handshaking and balancing the cups on the rimless saucers, eating and drinking was impossible.

In a small southern township I was entertained for a day by Ted Goetz and his family. At lunch Ted's mother said a very long grace. "Sorry about the long grace," said Ted's father. "But her food's worth waiting for."

"It's only just struck me," I said. "I've only been in the United States two months, but I've heard grace said in private houses more often than I would in Britain in two years."

Ted's father was a simple soul. "We more religious over here, huh?" he said.

"Well, I don't know," I said. "But in many ways you seem to take things much more seriously than we do, especially religious things."

"We do," said Ted. "In some ways, and in some places. See, lot of us round here, for instance, are descended from English Puritans. In Pennsylvania you get a lot of Dutch Baptists; Presbyterians in New England; Swedish Lutherans in Minnesota. All pretty serious folk."

But later Ted drove me round the town. As we cut through one of the side-streets, I saw a church, its name and the times of the services quivering in blue neon lights.

"Golly," I said.

"What's the matter?"

"That church," I said. "With the electric sign. It looks so odd."

"You have the names of your churches up, don't you?"

"Yes, but it's on a board or something."

"Well, what's wrong with having it in lights?"

"There's nothing wrong. It just made me say golly!"

We began to talk about Evelyn Waugh's novel, which describes some of the funeral parlours in California. "Ever seen one?" asked Ted.

"No."

"You shall. My uncle runs one."

"I don't think I'd care to."

"Don't you like American funeral homes?"

"I don't care for any funeral homes."

But we went. The only thing which distinguished the funeral parlour from the other houses in that pleasant street was a neon sign which said: "*The* Funeral Parlour." Inside, Ted's uncle sat in a very airy, luxuriously-furnished room, half office, half sitting-room. He looked far more cheerful than British undertakers do. "Come in," he said. "Make yourself at home."

When we left he gave me some of his cards. "Not much chance of you using them, I know," he said. "But you may be around again."

We drove on down the street, past a gently-sloping meadow, where some cypresses threw a purple shadow across the short green turf. "Lovely, that," I said, pointing.

"Glad you like it. That's where my grandmother's grave is."

"I thought you said we were going to have tea with her."

"Sure. She's not dead yet. But over here you buy a place for your grave from the guys who bury you—in advance. My folks have got theirs, too."

Back in his home Ted showed me some undertakers' advertisements. "Gosh," I said. "You'd think they were selling holiday cruises."

Ted rummaged through some current magazines. "Take a look at this," he said. He showed me a photograph of the calendar issued by one funeral parlour to its clients and prospective clients. On it was an extremely attractive young woman who wore no clothes. Her picture would have stood out in any G.I.'s collection of pin-up girls. "Beautiful in Death," ran the main caption.

"Whew!" I said.

"Isn't that something? Mind you, they don't all go so far."

That evening Ted drove me to meet Anthony and Edward, who were at the other end of the town. As we passed down the main street I saw what seemed a reassuringly familiar sight. Imitation Gothic pinnacles rose from an imitation Gothic nave. "Roman Catholic college run by the Jesuits," said Ted. As we passed slowly by the main gate, two black-robed figures emerged. For a moment I felt I was back in the Old World. Then I saw a poster on the wall, saying:

"GET IN THE SWING, FOR CHRIST THE KING!"

Another set of contradictions lies around the fact that Americans often seem sentimental, and often seem cynical. Sometimes they seem compassionate, sometimes they seem hard-hearted.

At one university, where people had asked questions showing deep sympathy with the people of Europe, I mentioned this to one of the professors. "What I can't understand," I said, "is why so many ordinary Americans can talk like that, and then so many of your Congressmen want to slash Marshall Aid, and talk as though Europe ought to make her own way. It seems to me like hypocrisy on the one hand, or faulty representation on the other.

"You've got it all wrong. It's neither."

"Well, what's the explanation?"

"Well, in the first place, the way our Senators and Congressmen talk is often very different from the way they act. You see, everything they say goes on 'the record.' Now when election times come round, if the average voter finds his representative has been advocating anything which is going to cost a lot of money, he gets suspicious. If, on the other hand, he finds his representative's been pleading for economy all along the line, he says: 'That's the man to represent me. They can't fool dollars out of him so easy.' An American always suspects the government of existing only to squeeze money out of him. You can't generalize about what the Americans are going to do by listening to what is said in Congress. Sometimes they just talk in Congress to see what people back home will say. They get to know pretty soon, I can tell you."

"They told me when I came to America it was a land of extremes," I said. "Very rich, very poor, very cold, very hot. And I can see too it's a land of surprises. You can't generalize."

"You can't—not safely. You've got so many different influences here, you see, and there's been so much space they haven't had to make very great efforts in adapting themselves to each other. There are all these different racial heritages you've heard about, their natural forces, like climate and geography. Mining in West Virginia, stock-raising in Texas, fruit-growing in California, lumbering in Washington State, small farming and fishing in Maine, you wouldn't expect to get the same kinds of life and the same kinds of characters in all those places, would you?"

"Of course," I said, "we've got local influences like that in Britain."

"Yes," he said. "But on such a small scale. With you it's localities, with us it's regions; tracts big enough to be countries in themselves. So much is different here, because it's so much bigger."

The professor looked hard at me. "By the way," he said. "When you go home and talk about the Americans, as I hope you will, and when you start to generalize, as I am afraid you will, don't make the most foolish kind of generalization of all."

"What's that?"

"If you see something over here which stands out in

your mind as being very different from what you've seen in Europe, don't assume that it exists over here because the American character is what it is, and that it doesn't exist over in, say, Britain because the British character is what that is."

"Right," I said, but I wasn't quite certain what he meant.

But I think I understood what he meant a few weeks later. I stood, once again, in New York, on the sidewalk of Fifth Avenue, watching the stream, the flood, of red and yellow streamlined taxi-cabs racing down the broad open streets between the tall skyscrapers. As far as the eye could reach, the road was straight; it looked more like a gently undulating racecourse than the main street of a modern city. As I stood there, one of New York's more friendly policemen strolled up.

"You English?"

"Sure—I mean 'yes.'"

"What d'ya think of it here?"

"I was just looking at this street," I said. "I was watching these cabs tear by, and then I thought of our taxis in London."

"Kinda slow, huh?"

"Yes," I said. "Compared with yours, they never seem to get out of bottom gear." And then I saw what the American professor had been getting at. "Of course," I said to the policeman. "It isn't that you're a faster people than we are. You don't go faster than we do because your minds are faster than ours, or because your character is different."

The policeman looked aggrieved. "But you just said we *was* faster."

"I said your cabs were faster than ours. But we could drive as fast as you Americans, and have just as fast cars if——"

"If what?"

"If they were any use to us."

"If they were any use to you?" He looked a bit bewildered.

"You couldn't use these things around Soho, and in the little streets round Chelsea, or for that matter in our little market towns. Everything's too small, the streets are too narrow."

"You oughta have 'em widened."

"We do widen some of them. But you wouldn't want us to pull down the Tower of London, or Westminster Abbey, would you, just so the traffic could go faster?"

"No, I guess not," he said. And I think he meant it.

He went off. I stood for a little longer, watching the crowd moving along the pavement. The people walked swiftly; they seemed to get where they were going much faster than the British would in Piccadilly Circus. But it was not because they were Americans, but because they had more room to stride along in. How freely and well they seemed to move—the pace of American life at its best. Yet there was nothing exclusively American about it. It was a pace at which all men could move if they built a world wide enough to take it.

CHAPTER XII

American Private Enterprise

PRIVATE ENTERPRISE in the United States is a living faith. When the frontier was the testing ground, the self-reliance of a self-made community immortalized itself under the title of "Rugged Individualism." Nowadays when the battle has moved into the economic sphere, it calls itself "Private Enterprise."

Two things go to make it. First the individual's pugnacity and courage, which his ancestors learned in saddle or covered wagon, or which bore them to a new rough plenty from the starving fields of Europe. Secondly, the belief that in the bountiful land of America there is nothing but opportunity for him who will go forward boldly and take it.

Opportunity. The American believes that it is there, for everybody. He is convinced of it.

To him the phrase "Private Enterprise" does not mean "Capitalism," "Exploitation," "Privilege" and the abuse of a handed-down unbridled power. It does not produce in him a deep-felt urge to rebel against a long history of economic repression. America knows little of this attitude; has had little of the experience which evokes it. Even in the memory of the living there have been some hard knocks. But they have not fallen often enough or stayed down long enough. America is young. She still trusts in her youth, in her hopes, her courage, in her opportunities. Fifty years hence she may not be in the same mood.

This faith in the American brand of Private Enterprise is not something which somebody invented and handed out to the masses like a religious creed or a political maxim. It is something which rises up out of the individuals, millions of them, who make up public opinion. The man in the street breathes it with his daily draught of American air. He exhales it through the nostrils of his political leaders. It inspires what they say at Washington, but its origin is on the New York sidewalk and in the fields of Oregon.

The red and yellow cab chugged slowly up the long, straight, snow-covered hill to Cherryville. My driver was a short, neatly-built fellow of about thirty-five. He wore a bright red shirt and a peaked cap, and a tight-fitting pair of whipcord breeches. Now and again he interrupted his flow of conversation to pick up the hand-microphone of his short-wave radio set and report his location to his boss.

"I cain't understand you British," he said at length.

"What can't you understand about us British?"

"You talk about having a government which represents the ordinary man in Parliament. Then those same guys go'n spend thousands of dollars on a royal wedd'n. On plush breeches, 'n horses 'n coaches and that kind of thing."

"It doesn't cost very much, really," I said. "The people like to honour the royal family, and they enjoy the colour, and the pomp, and the romance of the turnout. It's a great, and more or less cheap, treat for all London; and it reminds us of our great past."

"Waal. I reckon if you want money off us, like Mr. Acheson and Mr. Hoffman's always sayin' y'do, you oughta do without these treats. You oughta go easy on that past of yours."

I could see that, ahead of us, a big truck was reversing downhill.

"Not that I'm agin the British," went on the driver. I felt sure he hadn't seen the truck.

"I'm *for* the British," he went on. "I wanna marry a British girl. You know that?"

"No, I didn't know that. That truck up there's a big one, isn't it——?"

"I sure do. Do you know why? American women talk too much and they cain't cook. Give me—HEY! You son of a b——!"

The big truck swerved and we swerved, and in a second we had passed each other safely. "All right, you kin shut that door," said the driver. I put my legs back into the cab and shut the door again. "But if that big lug thinks he can do that to me——" he said wrathfully. Pulling his hat down hard on his head, he hopped out of his side and disappeared into the snow. Dimly through the frosted back window I could see him leaping up into the other truck's cab.

In about three minutes he was back. We proceeded up the hill. "You look pretty unscathed," I said.

"I look what?"

"You look as if either you haven't had a fight, or as if you had and the other chap couldn't put a finger on you."

"He didn't put a finger on me, and we didn't have a fight."

"Oh. I see."

"Don't think I'm afraid of getting a lickin'. Our local Union don't like us getting into fights."

"Would they have found out?"

"I'll say they would. That guy's on the local committee."

"What do you think of the Unions?"

"Waal, I don't rightly know. I think I'm agin 'em.

The good guys got to work along same as the bums. If you do too well, that ain't right. You cain't take your chances without some guy squawking. Yeah. I think on the whole I'm agin 'em. You got 'em in England?"

"Yes."

"What does the King think about 'em?"

"Well, I don't know. He certainly puts up with them."

"Uh-huh. Guess they get 'n his hair sometimes. Like they do in mine."

In the train from Newark to Philadelphia, a silver-haired, middle-aged man began to talk to me. "It's a pity you hadn't had really good Unions in Britain," he said. "It's not enough to strike. You must have leadership. You must show the owners ways out of their difficulties, be prepared to co-operate if they will, to give the answers, not think about destroying them. Otherwise you run on into Nationalization and State ownership, and all the rest of that stuff, Fascism and Communism." His thoughtful, lined, sympathetic face was earnest.

"You don't think Trades Unionism is a step towards Socialism, then," I said.

"Why, no, young man," he said. His voice quivered, he took his pipe out of his mouth and stared at me to see if I had meant what I'd said. "They'd have never made a Union man out of me if I'd thought that for a moment."

"Why are you a Trades Unionist?"

"Because I want to combine with equal and free men to protect myself against any advantage which an employer tries to take of me. I don't want to be against employers in general. I just want to be able to defend myself against those bullying ones that come along now and again."

On the other side of me was a much younger workman. At his feet he had the kind of can railwaymen or workers carry tea or coffee in. "Our Unions ain't for controls like yours," he said. "They're for freedom. We got 'em to fight for us, not to keep things gummed up quiet."

"Yes," I said. "I wouldn't say that 'quiet' or 'gummed up' is the impression a visitor gets of, say, Mr. Lewis."

"Sure. That's how we like it. All we want is a fair chance, and we got it in this country, brother. See that coffee-can there. The guy who owns the place where I work was taking a can like that to work in the train, only a few years ago. He used his chump, and worked hard. If I do the same, waal, I'll get where he is. I don't want no nationalization to stop *that* chance."

"Don't think me personal," I said. "But do we assume that our elderly friend here, who does not own his own business, has either not worked hard, or has not used his chump?"

"I just didn't have enough drive," said the silver-haired man with a sigh. "I had no ambition."

"See what I mean," said the young one with the coffee-can. "He admits it. He had no ambition. That makes all the difference."

"What's yours?"

"Mine? I want to have an outfit of my own. I want to get where the guy that I work for's got. I wanna be like him. Started off taking his can to work like me. Now he could write a cheque for a million dollars."

"Is he a good chap?"

"Well, I couldn't say."

"Is he a nice chap?"

"Search me. I never see him."

"Well, you say you want to *be* like him. What d'you know about him?"

"Waal, I don't know, I s'pose. 'Cepting he c'n write out a cheque for a million dollars."

There is no social protest against ownership in the United States. There is no class-consciousness in their wish to have a share of owning. There is no class to be conscious about, and the American does not want to share. He wants a fair chance to acquire the lot for himself.

Out in the countryside, many Americans hanker after their own plot of ground, their own house, their own piece of property. But in the big cities, millions of them seem to have no instinct for rooting themselves in solid, self-owned, permanent homes. Their enterprise and desire to get on expresses itself in spending their money on entertainments and accessories rather than on the accumulation of private property.

Halmar and Eunice lived in a couple of rooms they rented from Halmar's mother. Halmar was a semi-skilled workman; in the Army he had been a sergeant-driver. His wife had been to High School, and then took a short course in secretarial work. She was something in between a typist and a secretary. Between them they were earning £30 a week.

"That's big money, Halmar," I said. Halmar eased his bulk—he was born in Norway and weighed two hundred pounds—in one of his mother's chairs.

"It's not bad," he admitted.

"What are you going to do with it?"

"Jees, living's so expensive. A dollar for a hair-cut! And then we go out a coupla times a week, to the flicks, or on th'ice. Or I take Eunie to a night club—that's about thirty bucks a time."

"Do you save at all?"

"Not much. I cain't save at Christmas, 'cos I fans out the presents, and I cain't save in August 'cos me and Eunie takes a vacation. Last year we went to Cuba. Boy, is that a place. Cuba! Hummm." He rolled his eyes in a very un-Scandinavian manner. "And I cain't save around times like March, June, September and January 'cos I got to pay Ma the rent. So you can figure it out that I only saves in between times. See?"

"What d'you save *for*?"

"Well, me and Eunie wants to have an apartment of our own. You know, just a couple rooms, and a spare room, maybe. Then we figures on having a car. I've got my name down now, but I cain't possibly get one till 1949. Then Eunie wants a big radio, you know, one of them that turns the records over. There's one down in that store opposite the bus station. That machine is a honey. Oh, and then I wanna take lessons in golf."

"Golf?"

"Sure, why not?"

"But you seem so unsuited for golf." Halmar looked hurt. "I mean, Halmar, that a big strong young man like you looks too dynamic for that game."

"H'm, dynamic. That's an angle. Well, I figure golf's an elegant game. And all the business men play around here. If I wanna get on, Eunie says I gotta play golf."

"Don't you want to have a house of your own Halmar?"

"Oh, sure, some time. I ain't hurried. That'll have to wait. When the kids start coming along, they take up a lot of dough. Besides, an apartment's much more convenient."

At that moment Eunice came in. Tall, slim, and smart, her black eyes sparkled in their cleverly-painted mask. "I've had to change my stockings," she said. She extended a long, glistening, perfectly-moulded Manhattan leg. "Two bucks the pair," she said. "And sometimes I bust three pairs in a week. Ain't it awful?"

"Awful," I said.

Halmar got up from the chair which he was renting from his mother. The springs in the seat twanged with relief.

"There's another thing I'm saving for," he said. "Eunie and me wants to go back to Norway and see where our folks lived."

Many Americans owe their disinterest in rooting themselves to the soil to the fact that their roots still ache for land three thousand miles away.

It is mainly in the business of buying and selling, rather than in invention or production, that the keenest and most cultivated expressions of Private Enterprise are revealed. Americans will often throw their whole souls into lyrical salesmanship. One night Edward Boyle and I were walking down a street leading into New York's Broadway. Ahead of us we saw a crowd of people. They were overflowing from what seemed an arcade or a very wide shop entrance on to the pavement. We pushed our way in. At the other end of the broad opening into the shops was a platform. On it, with her back towards us, sat a girl whose figure was shown off to advantage by a closely-fitting black dress. Her thick golden hair hung freely down her back. At her side stood a tall young man in a well-cut suit. His voice was being amplified so that we could hear every word as though he were at our side. It was some time before I spotted the microphone. It fitted into his lapel button-hole, like a clip-on brooch or a membership badge. He was advertising some preparation for keeping the scalp clean and healthy, and the hair glamorous. We listened for about fifteen minutes. Then Edward Boyle said:

"I wouldn't care to try and rebut him."

I agreed. The young man's flow of speech, his wit, his eloquence, his swift, unerring feeling for the word that would amuse, now terrify, his audience was remarkable. He had no notes, and his jokes were obviously unprepared. His audience was spellbound. When he touched on the diseases which dirty hair could harbour, we stood and shivered. When he held up a cornucopia of the conquests we could make with our hair clean, we sighed and beamed. Women with Eton crops looked bitter, and bald men wept. When he looked round for his supply of packets of shampoo at fifty cents a time, only our feeling for the dollar gap was strong enough to spirit us away. As an orator he was better than any of the 150 debaters I heard in the United States.

Sometimes as one talks to Americans, one gets the feeling that since so much of their creative energy is already committed to the business world soon there may not be enough to keep their artists, writers and preachers reinforced with coming men. The physical and psychological stereotyped hygiene of their family and school life produces less and less of those rebels and eccentrics whose indifference to normality is such that they are ready to starve for art rather than make money in business.

"We're the greatest salesmen the world has ever seen," said one woman to me. "Our brassiere advertisements are so good that girls buy them who're too small to keep them on."

"That's fine," I said.

"Well, it's better to sell brassieres round the world than to go round with the Union Jack in one hand and a bayonet in the other."

"It's certainly better for the little girls," I said.

"Sure it is. We Americans can sell anything anywhere.

Naturally, we get our best men going into business. Especially the selling departments. Any fool can *make* a thing. What takes brains is being able to *sell* it when the customer's got one already."

"That takes brains all right."

"My son wants to be a writer. I tell him, 'Junior, you can be a writer in your spare time. You've got to eat first. You get yourself a job, and then start creatin'.'"

"What's he say to that?"

"He says, 'Ma, I've got a lot of creative energy. It won't *go* into business. I gotta write.'"

"What do you say?"

"I say, 'Private Enterprise can take all the creative energy that's going.' I tell him to go into advertisements. Plenty of writing, room for ideas, imagination, understanding what people want, and how to put things to 'em. Look at the poetry that goes into some of those ads for hard liquor. Even if he wanted to paint, look at those lovely pictures they paint for the railways and the flying, and all that kind o' thing. Isn't that so?"

"The only thing about the arts that go into ads," I said, "is that the communication is all on the same level, the mass level."

"What's wrong with that? This is a democracy, isn't it?"

"Yes. But sometimes the artist may have something special, all his own, to talk or paint about. And he must be free to put that across in his own way, even if it only reaches a handful."

"Sure, sure. I'm all for Junior being himself. I *say* to him, 'Junior, *be* different. But be different in your spare time. And when you've eaten.'"

Whether it is a sincere effort, and whether it will ultimately do any good, the American employer and the employee do try to keep the individual's identity alive.

In many shops, especially in the big cities, an assistant, after having served you, will give you a card with his name on it. Head waiters on trains, air-hostesses, taxi-cab men will do the same. In front of clerks at the bank, men at hotel desks, above the driver of the bus, on the counter of the dry goods store, will be a little placard saying whom you are dealing with. They will address you by your name within a second or two of the first opportunity they are given for learning it. "Very glad to see you at the hotel, Mr. Wedgwood Benn. And you, Mr. Harris. And *you*, Sir Boyle." Telephone operators, or switchboard girls at big apartment houses, who happen to have overheard your name, will make you glow with individual warmth by suddenly addressing you by it when you ring up an hour or so later. Service in America never tries to be impersonal. Whether out of spontaneous impulse or out of self-defence against the vast, engulfing anonymity of modern industrial life, the individual keeps his head up. And he tries to smile.

At San Francisco I had to buy the plane tickets. I walked in from the brilliant noontime sunshine into the long, cool, airy, elegantly-furnished Airways ticket office. At intervals down the long broad counter were the clerks. They were all young ladies, dressed in pale-blue linen costumes, with pretty little dark-blue forage caps set pertly on their heads. They all looked as if they had stepped out of a film. My turn for treatment came. I found myself in front of a girl with very blonde hair, big soft eyes and a naturally red mouth. Getting air tickets takes a long time, even at the worst of times.

"Do you have much air travel in England, Mr. Harris?"

"Yes. But it's rather different over there."

"It is? I'm not charging you for excess luggage by the way—you're a visitor. How's it different?"

"Thanks very much. Well, now, let me see. Well, I

don't think you'd wear a button-hole with your name on it, over there."

"I think that's bad. Don't you?"

"Well, I don't think it's very bad, really."

"Wouldn't you want to know my name in England, Mr. Harris?"

"Er—well. Er—yes, I wouldn't mind. Er—I suppose that if I wanted to complain about something you'd done it would be useful."

"I might do something nice for you. Wouldn't you want to know it then?"

"Dear me Er—yes, I never thought of that."

"Good-bye, Mr. Harris. Come back and see us."

They always say that. Hell! You wish you could.

The managements of many concerns in the U.S.A. print on their menus, bills or circulars, the hope not only that patrons will report inefficiency but any outstanding acts of courtesy and service. They single the individual out for praise as well as blame, and the individual certainly seems to respond to that treatment.

The belief in Private Enterprise is sometimes overpowering, especially in these days when Private Enterprise in Britain strikes them as being on what one debater called the "skids." The only way to cope with an excess of pugnacious American ego is to put on a bold face and hit back harder, and if necessary lower, than they do. They don't mind this. But if they think you have retreated skilfully, and from the safety of the next room or from behind the screen of British diplomacy are tittering at them, or being supercilious, they get very peevish. What is worse, they're liable to come bouncing in and demand a showdown.

We were travelling on the night train from somewhere in New York State to New York. We got on the train, very tired and short of sleep. We sat down in the restaurant car for a cup of milk before we went to bed. Suddenly I saw a big, broad-shouldered, husky American youth bearing down on us. His tie was one of the most flamboyant of those many patterns with which the more exuberant American offsets the general sameness of the rest of his clothes. "Hiya," he said.

If I had said "Hiya" back, he might have thought no more about us. But when I said "Good evening" he realized I was foreign.

"You French?" he said.

"No."

"Canadian?"

"British."

"Uh-huh. Over here at school?"

"Sort of. Debating."

"Been to Varnell University?"

"No."

"Gee, that's tough. Swell place. I was there. Sorry you couldn't make it. You'd 've seen something there. Where you bin?"

"Harvard, Yale, Princeton, Columbia——"

"Chop-houses. Gee, I'm sorry you couldn't make Varnell."

"Wish we could. It sounds a fine place."

"Best in the States. I was there."

"So you said. What did you study?"

"Hotel Management, chiefly. I filled in with Psychology. I'm doing my master's thesis right now."

"Collecting data?"

"You might call it that." It seemed that he was now working as assistant manager of an hotel in Illinois. He had sent a circular letter to a hundred hotel proprietors and managers in the south-west. With the circular letter went a questionnaire. About fifty had answered.

"What about the rest?"

"Bums."

On the basis of the fifty or so replies and his own practical experience in Illinois, he was writing the thesis. Eighty typewritten pages. He looked round the dining-car. There was something self-consciously professional about his scrutiny. "This place could do with some attention," he said, more in sorrow than in anger. "Look at that sugar. Been there days. And my coffee's cold. How's yours?"

"Drinking milk."

"Taste all right?"

"All right. Great treat for us to be able to drink milk when we like."

"It is? Oh, yeah, I get it. Things pretty bad over there, huh? All them rationing and controls. Waal, I guess you've asked for it."

"Of course we have," said Wedgwood Benn. "We elected the government that's doing it. And of course we asked for all the hardships which we knew came with a six years' full-blast war."

"Yeah. I know. It's too bad. I guess you got to face it: Britain's played out. It's too bad. Why don't you guys come over here and live?"

It was now that I learned the best way to deal with this kind of talk. "I don't want to leave Britain anyway," I said. "But if I did, the U.S. is the last place I'd come to."

There was a "clink" as our friend from Varnell dug his teeth into his coffee-cup. When his face appeared from behind it, it wore an expression of bewilderment, rather than annoyance. "You don't say?" he said.

"I've got nothing against America," I said. "It's a great country, with the warmest-hearted and most good-natured people in the world. There's masses of opportunity here. But the country's only got a future for young unmarried men."

"I'm married with two kids," he said.

"I'm married with three," I said, kicking Wedgwood Benn. "And I'd never dare to bring 'em over here."

"Gee! Why not?"

"I've heard too much about what this country went through in 1929, when there were fifteen million men unemployed, and big businessmen were shooting out their bankrupt brains all over the forty-eight States. I don't want to come over here, on the crest of this prosperity wave, and get into the 1929 kind of whirlpool in a few years' time. No, *sir*!"

He was beginning to look a bit dazed. I felt I was making ground. "Waal," he grunted sheepishly. "That's Private Enterprise. You gotta take the rough with the smooth. You can't have freedom without risk."

"I agree," I said. "But as I say, I'm a family man. *I* don't mind risks, but I'm not going to sit down in a few years' time and watch my kids suffer for *my* ideal of political and economic liberty."

"Well, there won't *be* a slump again," he said thickly.

"That's what they said in 1929," I said. "And you damn well know it. And what happened? No, I'll stay over in Britain. We may not all like the government, and we know we're all in for a pretty thin time. But at least we know where we stand. You say you're married?"

"Yeah."

"And with two children?"

"Yeah." He pushed his hair back from his forehead and passed his tongue over his lips. "And another one on the way."

"You'd better chuck that thesis quick," I said, "and come over to Britain while the going's good."

"You British tie a guy up," he said. "You make my head go round. I'm off to bed."

"Good night, then."

"Good night."

He didn't say "Come back."

As a matter of fact, there *are* people leaving the United States because they think that other places are better. At Washington the three of us wandered on our own around the Senate House. A young policeman came up. "You can't go in there," he said.

"Sorry. We'll go back."

"Are you gentlemen English?"

"We are."

"That's different. Now, if you'd like a quick walk round I'll take you."

He was very kind. He took us to see some of the interesting sights, the Senate Chamber, the library, and the President's little retiring-room. We began to notice that he spoke with more fluency and knowledge than most policemen would be likely to have. We fished about a little and then we discovered the reason. He was a part-time policeman. With the money he earned for keeping order he was buying himself education at the local university.

"Will you go on being a policeman when you finish at school?"

"No, I don't think so."

"What are you going to do?"

"I'm not certain. But I'm thinking of going to Australia."

"For a trip?"

"No, for good. There's not enough scope in this country. Things are tightening up."

Sometimes you come across Americans who regret that the individualism and enterprise of the American is directed so much into industry, into buying and selling, and away from property and the land. In one of the southern states I met an old farmer. He lived in a grey stone house with a dark-blue slated roof. Peacocks strolled on the grass lawns between the small privet hedges. There was an iron seat on some of the red gravel paths, and over the palings the park stretched away between the widely-planted round-topped oaks. It might have been England if the day had been in April instead of January.

"Don't think all Americans are like your Halmar and Eunice," said he. "Lot of us still as keen on the land, on having our own homes, and our own plots as ever we were."

"Oh, yes, I don't doubt that."

"Sometimes I think you British do. Lot of you talk about your landed aristocracy, landed gentry, the yeomen, and the good old English peasant and his rod, pole, or—what in hell's the other?"

"Perch."

"That's right, perch—as if nobody else ever had an acre to love and call his own. The only people who really got any right to talk about loving the land, and caring for the home, are th' people who've had to fight for it—not somebody else's home, y'understand, but their own. Fought for it, against fire, flood or armed men, and maybe seen it burn, or wash away, or the barns be pulled down brick by brick."

"Like the people in London."

"Exactly. Or some of them Russians. I'd hang every Red I got my hands on, but I think there's a lot of Russians who love their homes and their bit of soil a lot more'n many Americans. Or British. What d'you say?"

"I say yes."

"Down here we understand the land. Up there 'n the north, they don't. You've heard about the Civil War?"

"Yes. I saw a film called *Gone With the Wind* which was all about it. Was it anything like that?"

"It was. But the real war wasn't in Technicolor. What you British got to remember is that the war's only just finished. In some cases it *ain't* finished. There's still too many people alive who can remember. Anyway, that's off the point. Now, my father came back here and found this place flat and ashes. Just like in that film. He came back with some horses. He'd lost eighteen, but he had two left. He was considered a very lucky man. He came limpin' down that road there, just like it may be in that film. And he started to build up from the start again. Now why did he do that?"

"Well, because he wanted to."

"I want to go out steeple-chasing, but I cain't."

"Well, he felt he ought to."

"I oughta be nice to my son-in-law, but sometimes I cain't be, the durned fool."

"Well, I don't know."

"O' course you don't. You're too young. He did it because he *had* to. Just like an animal gits itself a burrow, or a bird the nest, my father had to get down to it and build up the kind of home he used to have, and get the land like it used to be. Lots of folk didn't succeed like he did, but they had a try."

"And folks to-day don't try?"

"That's it. They don't try. But why don't they try?"

"Er—I don't know."

"Because they ain't got that instinct any more. It's been bred out of them. D'you know what's doing it?"

"You tell me, sir," I said.

"*Private Enterprise!*"

"Let me get this straight, now," I said. "All over the last twenty-five states I've been in, I'm told that Private Enterprise is making America what she is to-day."

"Sure. That's what I'm telling you. And a damn bad place she is."

"That's what the Senate Committee would call 'Un-American talk.'"

"It's plumb *good* American talk. And I'd like to hear some lazy good-for-nothing Senator tell me otherwise. Take it from me, this talk of Private Enterprise's one of the biggest hunks of humbug we Americans have ever fallen for. And we certainly have fallen for some humbug. It's another of them Yankee tricks."

"If you don't mind, I'll use that point in the next debate."

"Go ahead. But get it right. The failure or the greatness of this country, or any other country, won't depend on how many men will be saying: 'I believe in Private Enterprise.' It'll depend on how many men don't need to rely on anybody else for their food and shelter. To-day a few big financial harpies encourage more and more ordinary men to leave the land for the city, and what's more to the point, to leave the land life for the city life. 'Stead of spending his energies on producing food and establishing a home, he goes off to apartments in a great prison of a city, takes high wages for poisoning himself to death and for losing all th' ability God gave him of doin' and makin' with his wits and hands. How does he spend them high wages? On keeping himself sufficiently amused to keep alive—radio sets, cinemas, baseball games and cocktail bars. How much does he ever come to own? Half of what he does and uses is got on credit. Hire purchase and the like. Yet when you start attacking the centre of this disease, people start shouting 'Hands off Private Enterprise.'"

"What is the centre of the disease, then," I asked.

"Credit. A few big bankers are always mortgaging the whole damn country, tho' don't forget, young man, a mortgage is a mortgage even when the state takes it out. They put down enough loans to encourage industry to go full out. Industry churns out wages, and everybody gets a job. Once everybody gets a job everybody starts buying things hire-purchase. Why, in 1929 the whole durn country was using things which it had promised to pay for with perhaps two years' labour per head. Living on credit. On tick. Mind you, I don't blame the men that work. I blame the big guys who encourage them into thinking that that's the American way of life. Son, I'm telling you it's the American way of death. I don't say Americans invented it, and I know other countries suffer from the same complaint. But we're the folk that's giving that system it's great, all-time workout."

"Well," I said. "It's certainly a change for me to hear Private Enterprise talked of like this."

"Private Enterprise as a phrase oughta be abolished. It ain't private, and it ain't got no enterprise. It just means a chance for the few to make fools of the many. Stops 'em having the only real thing that makes freedom mean anything at all in a real kind of way—a piece of ground to call your own, and the time and the inclination to make it bear fruit. You've got to have the right instinct for that, son. And how can good Americans have that instinct when Private Enterprise, if it ain't watched carefully, is goin' to destroy it. Private Enterprise just now's going to mean electric washers for the million on the hire-purchase system, and only one man in a thousand living a natural life."

He spat on the turf. "And there's one other thing about the land," he added.

"What's that."

"It's a language. It links men all over this planet in a way that using the same words in the same tongue *cain't* do. What's the use of a Cockney engine-driver and a Manhattan stockbroker being able to speak English. They ain't got nothing in common to talk about. There's more chance of a Russian peasant and a labourer from Iowa getting together and getting along. Industries change, and the problems of manufacturing and pro-doocing make men think differently at different times. But if we all get back on the land, stand on something solid that's common to us all, then I reckon the different countries'll knock along better than they do right now."

CHAPTER XIII

Americans and "Class"

AFTER the debate at Evans College we went back to one of the Fraternity houses. The cellar was got up to resemble a Pig and Whistle bar, though the beer came out of cans. We started singing songs. One American boy sang a ditty which Sid Field made famous, and another gave a good imitation of Stanley Holloway reciting "Albert and the Lion." The three Oxford men delivered "Green Grow the Rashes, O!" Then Edward Boyle branched out on his own and sang the "Eton Boating Song."

After this we began to talk. Eton took us to "Public Schools," which we had to explain were really private, and talking of schools took us to the "Old School Tie."

"In the war," said the boy who had imitated Stanley Holloway, "I heard that all your officers had to have been to your private—I mean 'public'—schools. Is that so?"

"No. I was an officer myself. I went to an ordinary state school."

"Well, anyway," said a boy in a black and white lozenged sweater. "Leaving the army out of it, I reckon that, by and large, there's a lot more class in Britain than there is over here."

"What do you mean by class?"

"Well, I reckon that when a country's got 'class,' the people in it tend to get divided up into layers. For instance, labourers and manual workers on the bottom, tradesmen and professional men in the middle, folks with land and big-shot business-men on the top."

"But you can't *do* that, Johnnie, you dope——"

"Will you hush up? I've not finished. Well, when a country's got class, I reckon most of the people in those layers have a kind of common way of thinking and feeling about politics, and religion, and art. They even have common manners, tend to wear the same kind of clothes and eat the same kind of food. Each layer has a kind of common attitude to the other layers—envy, maybe resentment going up; patronage, and maybe a little contempt, coming down. Now, I know that sounds pretty arbitrary, and I know it don't work out so obvious as that. But I reckon you've still got something like that over in Europe, and I reckon we haven't got it over here."

"Baloney," said the boy who had imitated Albert. There was a long wrangle among our hosts to which the British listened with interest. A tall boy with the fashionable close-cropped hair came over and sat next to me. His suit of grey flannel was dark, almost black. The jacket was low in the skirt and cut with a fine sense of line. His trousers were narrow, no more than eighteen inches where they touched his dark, neat, hand-sewn English leather shoes. He was a very, almost formidably, elegant young man.

"I don't know much about 'class,'" he said, his tone chipping out inverted commas for the word, "but there's a good deal of snobbery in this country. Come along and see the play we're putting on to-morrow night. It's set a few years back as far as time goes, but it's still a good social document, and it's amusing."

The following night we had to take part in a radio discussion, and we only saw a few minutes of the play. We arrived just in time for the first punch: the wealthy and aristocratic New England father was being informed that his son was about to marry the daughter of a man who lived in Kansas. He had to be helped to a chair. The daughter's father had lashings of money, and the girl was sweet. But they lived in Kansas. "*Kansas!*" he whispered. They poured brandy down his throat to keep him breathing.

"See what I mean," said the boy in the dark grey flannel suit. He himself had the soft sophisticated voice of New England.

"What the hell did he have against Kansas, anyway?"

"It was new."

"New! What about the whole of the United States?"

"Well, there you are. Perhaps that's the reason: what *is* old over here we hang on to like grim death—there's so little of it to breed from. The oldest British families go back to the Norman Conquest. Here we can only make the *Mayflower*, but those who can make it, well, they make it big."

A few days later I went to have a drink with the leading lawyer in what would correspond to a medium-sized market town in England. My host, John Heinz, met me at the door. His jacket was off, and his tie was loose. "Kind of warm," he said. "Slip your jacket off." I followed him into the big sitting-room, where two young friends of his were sitting. Both men had their jackets off. One of them was drinking a high-ball, the other held to his lips a bottle of Coca-cola. It was straight out of the ice-box, so he had wrapped a paper table-napkin round the bottom.

John was keen on the theatre, and I told him about the play I saw at Evans. "It's a good play," he said, chuckling. "And pretty true."

I told them about the discussion in the Evans' Pig and Whistle.

"Class over here is so different from what you Europeans have been used to," said John. "Over there, there were two dominant ideas for a long time: the idea of Breed, and the idea of Station. I guess you had them both worked out in the old feudal system. At the top of the community, you had the aristocrat, the man of blue blood, the man of family, who owned the land and married the sisters and daughters of men like himself. Below him you had a whole scale of classes, with the serf and the house-servant at the bottom. Everybody had his place, and the aim of everybody was to do as well as he could *in* that place."

"Horrible," said the young man with the Coca-cola.

"Sure," said John. "But that state of affairs kept Europe in shape for a mighty long time. It was a phase she went through, and I guess it served a pretty important turn."

"Thank God we didn't have to go through it," said the man with the Coca-cola.

"Well," said John. "There it is. This country got started just about when Europe was dumping that old feudal-family-class system on the heap. We started off here with the idea that men were equal. And of course, in a new country, where all that matters is whether you've got the guts to go out to the frontier and fight for your patch of land, and the grit to till it and stock it till it bears fruit, I guess who your father was and whether you talk like in a land-owner's accents don't matter so much. Or *didn't* matter so much."

"It still doesn't matter," said the Coca-cola man stoutly.

"Mind you," said John, "I'm not saying that that kind of thing still matters in Europe. But though the kind of society where it did matter may be broken up or altered even a hundred years ago, the memory, the habits of thought, the various senses of inferiority and superiority may hang on. Sometimes they come out in the manners, the bearing, even the appearance of individuals. See what I mean?"

"I think I do, John," said the boy with the high-ball. His voice was good-natured and slow. He lay back comfortably in his chair with his hands folded on his chest. "I spent a lot of time in London during the war," he said. "Sometimes I'd go into one of your high-class restaurants. Most of the people'd come in pretty much at ease, looking dressed for the place, and talking in the same kind of accent. Then perhaps another couple'd come in. You'd only got to watch the way the waiter'd treat them to see that they, well, didn't belong. I don't mean he'd do a bum job for them; he'd just not put on the full act. This couple would sit there, and you could see they didn't know whether they were enjoying themselves or not. She'd be wondering whether she had the right kind of dress for the joint, and he'd be wondering how much he'd tip the waiter. You'd see him give the guy about twice as much as he need, even if he were Rockefeller. D'you get the kind of picture?"

"Yes," I said. "But doesn't that happen in all countries?"

"Sure, in its different ways I suppose. But over here, if you've got the money, the place is yours. People stride into a restaurant like they know that. If a guy did get a bit out of his depth he'd be more likely to take a sock at the head waiter than leave too big a tip."

I went back to New York by the subway. Opposite me sat two young men who looked like university students. ". . . So you see," said one of them, "you only need to introduce the equation, P equals r^2 Cosine A, when you do without the constant." My glance fell on a little man sitting next to them. He looked up at the young men from his paper and stopped chewing his gum. "... On the other hand," went on the student, "you can use Heine's refractive indices, and work it out in logarithms."

"Is zat so?" said the eyes of the little man. When we got out we passed through the train door together. "Wonderful thing, Si-yence," he said.

"I didn't understand a word of it," I said. "I wish I did."

"Why didn't you ask 'em?"

"Well, I suppose I didn't like to?"

"Won't learn like that, bud. Where'd old Einstein be if *he* 'didn't like to'?"

"Did you understand it all?"

"Not me."

"Well, why didn't *you* ask?"

"I di'n't wanna know. I just like the sound of them si-yentific words."

As we reached the sidewalk a big black roadster slid up. The man driving it was wearing a well-cut grey birds'-eye suit. A gold watch twinkled on his wrist. On her fur coat lapel the lady by his side wore a diamond clasp. The man leaned through his window. "Could you tell me the way to the docks from here?" he asked. His tone was friendly but crisp.

The little man was looking at the woman with an appraising stare which she met without embarrassment. "Go down three blocks, then turn left," he said. He leaned with one arm on the door and his foot resting on the running-board. He had his pipe in his hand, and for a second looked as though he was going to tap it out on the bonnet. "Go easy with the speed down there, brother," he added. "The cops round here is mighty busy."

"O.K. Thanks a lot."

The car purred off. "Get *her*?" asked my companion. "Jees, what a doll!"

In the cool comfortable lounge of the Harvard Club, the green-shaded standard lamps cast a mellow glow on the leather chairs and polished tables. From the score or so members sitting talking or playing backgammon rose a good-humoured hum. Now and again there came a hearty laugh. Sometimes a hand slapped a broad back. "Why, you old so-and-so," came from a group of smartly-dressed professional men. Members coming in or out exchanged brief outspoken conversation as they passed each other at ten yard's range. There was no snuffling around one another, no fear of seeing and of being cut. They called out sharp and clear. If the other man didn't hear they shouted again: "Hey!"

I leaned back against the bar, balancing in my hand one of the leather dice-shakers with which the counter was supplied. "Come on, young man, roll 'em," said a voice. It was an elderly gentleman who had given me a lift in his car the night before.

"I wonder what would happen if somebody introduced dice into the Athenaeum," I said.

"I guess somebody'd complain," he said. "Some folks don't like to see 'em here. Is this place like the clubs in London?"

"In some ways."

"Main difference?"

"More cheerful."

"We've got some pretty morgue-ish ones too," he said. "But on the whole I think you British, especially the more educated ones aren't as easy-going as they are over here. More shy, you know, more inhibited in company." I told him what John Heinz had said about the traces of class-consciousness in Britain. "Sure," said my elderly friend, "that helps. I don't say that British self-consciousness is the same as class-consciousness, but I think there's a connection between the two. Now I don't say that there's no class over here, but there's certainly less class-consciousness."

"Why?"

"Partly because, as your friend said, we started off here more or less from scratch. Partly because of the shape of family life over here. See, if you're not a very poor white over here, or a negro, and if you're not in the upper crust, the life you lead over here is basically the same as anybody else's."

"A much bigger middle class?"

"That's it. The middle class is our 'masses.' As long you're not in one of the two extremes, how you spend your money, what kind of a house you live in, what kind of school environment you have, what kind of entertainment you have is all basically the same. If you're a garage hand you sit in the cheap seats at the theatre, and when you own a bus company you take a box. But you see the same kind of show. My office-boy has a fifty-dollar gramophone at home—mine cost ten times as much. But our kids play the same discs. There are only two kinds of manners over here: good ones and bad ones. Now in England, from what I hear, your manners depend on how you lived, where you went to school, and a few other things."

"I've certainly noticed the sameness of the manners over here," I said. "All the students I've met have got a lot more self-possession than ours in Britain seem to have."

"Sure, and if you got to know as many of the working-class kind of people over here, you'd find *they* seem a lot freer, more self-possessed and bolder than they are in England. Mind you, I'm not saying that they *are* those things: we're discussing manner, appearance."

He caught sight of a young man walking by. "Hullo there, Jim. How've you bin?"

"Hullo, Judge. I'm fine. How're you?"

"I'm fine. Say 'Hullo' to your Dad for me, will you?"

"O.K., Judge."

The boy disappeared into the reading-room.

The judge turned to the bartender. "Give us a couple more Scotches, Jack," he said. He puffed at his cigar for a moment or two. "There's another reason why the workers over here seem to be more self-confident, less class-conscious, than they are—or used to be—in Europe. There's been no political class struggle over here, no long-term attempt by one level of property-owners to claim the right to vote which had been once monopolized by the higher level. The atmosphere of this country is free of that kind of thing, whereas over there you've still got memories of it. That's a fact that cuts both ways though. It's the struggle for rights, and then the struggle to preserve them, which keeps a people politically conscious. That's why you in Britain are more advanced politically than we are. That's why over here the worker hasn't formed a political party of his own. You've got the remains of the class struggle to keep politics still personal and vital to the man in the street. Over here he's been free so long, it doesn't mean so much to him, and consequently he's slack about taking an interest in the way he's governed."

"You said there were two reasons why your workers seem more self-confident and self-possessed than ours," I said. "What's the other one?"

"Every worker here knows—or believes—that if he works hard, he can make more money. Most people in this country believe that money, extra dollars, is the only thing that makes one man different from another. As long as the man in the street, the man on the bottom, believes that he has as good a chance as the next man to get to the top, to get more of the only stuff that takes you to the top, then he won't talk too much about class or feel too much about it."

"I suppose this money business is the reason why so many Europeans go away from here with the idea that all the Americans care about is money."

"Sure. Though, of course, we don't hear that so much since Marshall Aid began. However, money does go a long way in this country and it goes right to some people's heads. Don't think it's because we're all that materialistic. We're not. You see, we haven't birth to boast about, and we don't have honours like knighthoods and peerages. Money's the only 'honour' most of us know of. And there's another side to money over here. A lot of people genuinely believe that making money is a sign of moral as well as economic success. You know the kind of view—those who live virtuously make money, the poor are poor because they deserve to be. There are thousands of people over here who never forgave F. D. Roosevelt for introducing unemployment relief in the early thirties, not because they didn't want to pay up but because they thought they were being asked to act against their religious principles."

Another man walked up to the bar. "Hullo, Judge."

"Why, hullo, Tom. How've you bin—how's Elsie?"

"Well, she's better now, but I want to get her away. The house is too darned big without any help, and I just can't get any for her."

The judge turned back to me. "That's another thing," he said. "Over in Europe I guess you had people who were brought up to feel that working for somebody else, washing their dishes and waiting at table, was the natural thing, the ordained thing. Over here, you can't get many people who'll put up with that and call it a job. If you manage to get hold of somebody for a house-servant, well, you daren't say too much to him in case he gets cross.

And of course he doesn't act in a very servant-like way—not by European standards. He talks back at you, refers to your wife as 'your wife,' or 'the missus,' in front of guests, and says 'O.K., chief' when you ask for the dinner to be served." He laughed. "I'm exaggerating but you know what I mean." He looked at his watch. "I've got to go to Fifty-fifth Street. Can I give you another lift?"

We put on our coats and walked to the front door. In a moment we were in a red and yellow taxi. "You know," I said to the judge, "it's all right for young chaps like us, but lots of elderly British people must get a bit of a shock when they come to New York and the taxi-man calls them 'bud.'"

"Ah, well," said the judge, leaning back on the cab cushions. "There it is—it's all part of the picture here. Compared with yours I guess in many ways our country is pretty raw. Our manners, like our law and our politics, they've got their rough sides. Culture over here is still camping out. You see, it's a young country. We've just got to wait for it all to grow up."

"I suppose you have."

The judge turned and looked at me. "Mind you, son," he said. "Being young, it has its advantages, and roughness often goes with independence. You may be able to kid an American into thinking he's his own master when he isn't, but whenever he recognizes an attempt to dominate him, he won't stand for it. He'll get tough. And he's willing to get tough on other people's behalf as well as his own. I know you British will appreciate that."

"We've had good cause to."

"And talking about Britain," said the judge, "reminds me of how difficult it is to generalize about these things. 'Britain the home of freedom,' 'Britain never shall be slaves,' 'Britain, democracy's outpost'—we've always been hearing these things, and we've never disbelieved them. Yet, if my clients on Fifth Avenue want a really docile servant, they send over to Britain for one."

"H'm," I said. "That's interesting. But what does that prove?"

"Proves nothing, of course," said the judge. "But it certainly makes one think. Here you are, son, Fifty-fifth Street. And mind how you step."

CHAPTER XIV

American Negroes

ONE of our debates was against Green University. It was a university for negroes. We arrived on Friday afternoon. In the absence of the president, our week-end was arranged by his wife. Her pale brown olive-tinted face was dotted with attractive freckles. Her features were soft and fine, her eyes dark, but bright and sparkling in a Spanish rather than a negroid way. Her face and gestures were her chief characteristic, and in these she out-charmed many a sophisticated white hostess we had been honoured by.

Not intellectual, but with a swift and strong female intelligence, she knew exactly what she wanted. There were few minutes to ourselves at Green. Continually we were either seeing or being seen. We, representatives of a foreign white race, were to see the promise and potentiality of the American negro. And people from the local white universities were to see us seeing it.

The Debate Hall was packed out, about five hundred people sitting in a space meant for a hundred. They sat two on a seat, crouched on the floor, sat between the legs of tables. The sea of black faces shone like ebony in the lights. With so many people in such a small hall the atmosphere was electric. The chairman was a local negro barrister. He sat between us and the Green team, and just before he began his introductory address trembled so much that the small table quivered. One of the debaters wore an elegantly-pointed beard and gold pince-nez; the other had soft, slumbering eyes and shoulders like a bull. The British were to propose that basic industries should be nationalized. The negroes were to oppose it. The usual debate procedure was altered slightly. Behind the negro pair sat about eight young negro men and women who, after the main speeches, were to fire questions at us. Behind us sat about the same number who were to do the same against our two opponents.

The two negro speakers put up every possible argument for Private Enterprise. No white debater we heard had been more eloquent on its behalf, none more ready to blow the trumpet of American individualism. After the four main speeches, a shower of sharply-pointed questions was hurled at us. We hoped for support from our second line, but to our dismay we found that only four of them were really on our side. The other four were throwing a barrage of out-and-out socialist arguments across at our opponents, and we were being transfixed, as it were *en passant*, for being too weak-kneed to advocate a thoroughgoing programme. Then, queries and criticisms poured in from the front of the house, shot in between the hinges of the doors, from where an overflow of a hundred unseen, but far from unheard, listeners sat out on the stairs. Questions parachuted down from the tops of cupboards, enfiladed from the windowsills, and exploded under the chairs we sat on. Private Enterprise at its most reckless, Communism at its most sweeping, all kinds of political opinion flamed and cannonaded above the heads of the debaters and the perspiring chairman.

There were all shades of colour in the room. All kinds of face and hair, all tones to the American accent. Behind me two negro girls leaned forward in their seats, their faces animated and their eyes flashing as they tore Private Enterprise into accurately chosen and resounding shreds. One was dark; the other was of that dusky shade associated with the South Sea islands. Tall, graceful, willowy, full-lipped creatures, both were packed full of brains and quick thinking.

After it was all over we felt very limp. I went round to have some coffee with the young man in charge of the literature department. He was about thirty, tall, with a sallow complexion and thick spectacles. Only his frizzyish hair made him look a negro. His voice was cultured and soft, light and quick in tone and pace. We sat and talked about poetry in the United States, on negro poetry in particular. His own verse had been published in leading magazines. He was witty and kind and splendid company. His wife was black as pitch, her hair in tight ungovernable curls, her big white teeth flashing in the lazy smile of the traditional Topsy. Her voice was like a flute and her gracious mind looked straight out through her shining eyes.

On the Saturday night we went to hear the university choir sing carols. About a hundred of them stood packed closely on the stage. It was strange to see the dark faces and black clasped hands against the familiar white of the surplices. Their singing was most moving; it had that not-of-this-world quality which a Celt hears in the choral singing of the Welsh miners. The solos were sung with great feeling, and with a memorable standard of technique. A pompous white conductor sawed the air with his baton and rolled his eyes at the diminuendos like a tipsy old woman.

Half-way through the service we paused for prayer. The chaplain delivered it from the pulpit. Silver-haired and light-skinned, his eyes and his soft kind voice were his only negroid attributes. We prayed long and hard for blacks and whites without discrimination. The prayers were extempore and often naive. ". . . And let us remember William Robinson who fell off his ladder this afternoon, while he was decorating the clock above the doors, O Lord, and had to be taken away to hospital, and cannot be with us to-night. . . ." Silently, on our knees, we prayed for William Robinson.

Next morning we walked about the university, looking at their theatre, their laboratories and their libraries. The negroes at Green seemed to have all the departments you would find at a white university. But each was smaller, more primitive, and needed about ten times the funds it had to make it as good as the departments I saw at Rocky. The books in the library were tired-looking, and the reading-rooms were dingy. Culture was winning, but she was having to put up a fight.

"We can't complain," said one young medical student. "After all, we could go to one of the white universities where negroes are accepted as students. There are many who do."

"Why do you come here, then?"

"Well, two reasons I guess. One is that it's nice to have a kind of holiday from that long feeling I've had while being educated in other places, that I'm on my own, on sufferance, if you know what I mean. Also, as places like this exist, it's up to negroes to support them, keep them going, put the best black brains and efforts into making them a success."

"D'you think there ought to be more of these universities?"

"I reckon that until we get really accepted at white ones, *feel* sufficiently at home to be able to work there, these places are vital to us. Though of course, it means that our colour-consciousness is maintained."

"Tell me," I said. "How do you negroes get on together here."

"Like most other people, I guess," he said. "Some of

the lighter-skinned negroes look down on the darker-skinned ones; and some of the prouder negroes will resent others being too obsequious with white folk. Oh yes, there's plenty of tensions among students here. But that's not because they're negro, you understand. It's because they're human beings. Their ordinary human jealousies, hopes and fears happen to work themselves out in terms of colour instead of nationalism, or political ideology, or religion or some other rational organization of instincts."

"Any chance of getting more money for negro education," I asked.

"I don't know. After all, if America is going to spend money on helping British industry she can't spend that on the negroes as well."

We left on the Saturday afternoon, after helping the president's wife to decorate her drawing-room with evergreen. "Our only regret," said Wedgwood Benn, "is that we've missed your husband. If he's going to be at Georgetown for that education conference perhaps we could see him. Perhaps he'd come and have lunch with us at the hotel."

His wife neatly cast a loop of evergreen about the top of the ivory crucifix above the mantelpiece. "You'd have to go and have lunch with *him*," she said. "He's not allowed in white hotels in Georgetown."

* * * * *

Outside the slow, bumping train the sun poured down on the untidy scenery of Florida. Palms and yellow pine were draped with soft masses of creeper; a bright-plumed bird flashed screeching through the brush, its image mirrored in the stagnant pools along the track. Nature looked and smelt hot, damp and slightly sticky. One longed for the tang of the sea, or a great mid-west wind to blow away this mouldering unhealthy beauty. The train lumbered on half-heartedly.

The man next to me and myself finished our fresh Kadota figs simultaneously. The negro waiter brought us on the same dish an egg, two pieces of crisp streaky bacon, a waffle with syrup on it, and on the edge of the plate a small paper cup of marmalade. We drank our coffee out of the thick, stodgy china cups, which gives American coffee the full, gross touch on the lips which, as much as the cream in it, gives it a different taste from that of the British.

My companion suddenly saw me staring over his shoulder. "What's up?" he said.

"That curtain. They're putting up a curtain across that end of the diner."

"Sure; for the negroes."

"Why?"

"We don't have separate dining-cars for white people on this route, so they curtain off about a third of the car."

"I haven't seen that done before."

"That means you haven't been in the South before. See, segregation and the colour bar varies a great deal, depending on where you are. Up in the north, New York, say, or over on the west coast, in Los Angeles, the negroes get treated very much like white folks. Well, perhaps that's exaggerating. But you know what I mean. They can sit next to white folks in the theatre, or at school, in the train, and so on. But down here in the South, though even the South varies, you get two sets of everything! Two schools, two railway coaches, two toilets, two entrances to public buildings, and two separate parts of the same town for both to live in."

"A negro quarter?"

"That's right. Some of 'em ain't too comfortable, of course. Lots of that kind of thing."

He pointed out at the tattered tropical scenery that was limping past the window. In a clearing of what looked like a thin silver-birch wood, stood two battered and sodden-looking shacks. They were square and brown, a low verandah running along the weather-stained front, a wisp of smoke mounting from a crazy stove-chimney. A mean and mangy-looking yellow dog was gnawing at a stale and meatless bone. Two half-naked children played listlessly in the sun. In the porch an old gnarled negro sat back gently swaying in a ricketty rocking-chair.

"Florida. The playground of the world," said my companion. "By the way, don't think that only negroes live like that in America. The 'poor whites' are almost as badly off in some places."

"Poor whites?"

"Used to mean the small landholders who didn't own any slave labour, pushed on out on their own, then became small tenant farmers and share-croppers as each generation found it harder to get along. Now you might call 'em peasants. Some of 'em are awful poor, even to-day." He was pushing back his chair. From his waistcoat pocket he pulled a long, slim, tightly-rolled cigar. "Funny thing," he said. "Europeans pay a lot of money to get Havana-rolled cigars. I pay a small fortune to get these rolled in Piccadilly. Y'know, one half of the world doesn't know what the other half's doing."

"Where exactly would you say the 'South' *is* in the United States?"

"A very practical question, son, most Americans don't know either. Very difficult to give an answer and definition's liable to give trouble."

"In that case," I said. "Give me the shortest."

"O.K. The ten states below the survey line made a coupla hundred years ago by Mason and Dixon. Let me see now, Virginia, North Carolina, South Carolina,

Georgia, Florida, Alabama, Tennessee, Mississippi, Arkansas and Louisiana. Yeah, that's fair enough."

"Where's the 'Deep South'?"

"Waal, I reckon, roughly speaking, Georgia, Alabama and Mississippi. Some pretty bad places there, both for treating negroes and for white poverty."

"What's this business about 'passing the line'?"

"Sometimes a guy's negro blood gets so thinned out he looks more like a white man than a black man. When that happens, he's 'passed.' D'you want to see one?"

"Yes."

"Right. We'll walk back through the diner to the smoking-car. You look at the waiter with the white hair."

We strolled through the dining-car. There were five dark-skinned, crisp-haired negroes. But there was a sixth waiter who looked like a white man. His long silky white hair, his rich, full, dark eyes and his sensitive mouth made him look more like an aristocratic Italian than an American negro.

"See him?"

"Yes. But I wouldn't have spotted him myself."

"Nine Americans out of ten wouldn't have. But no negro would miss him, nor anybody who's lived with negroes a lot, like me."

"Do negroes want to 'pass'?"

"That waiter didn't seem to want to. A lot do. Whether it's because they really want to join in the kind of society they see white guys enjoying, or just because they're so scared of being pushed around, and being knocked around in some localities, it's hard to say."

"I suppose life's easier if you can pass," I said.

"Yes. But I know negroes, not the very dark ones, of course, who can get away with a lot without passing. If one guy I know gets to a town where the hotels won't take negroes, he puts a scarf round his head, goes up to the desk, says he's a Moslem and his name's Ram Dam Hickory from Bermuda, and gets a room. If the hotel's a bit swell, he says he's an Indian prince."

We arrived at Comodo. I swung myself and my suit-case off the high Pullman platform into the sunshine. The atmosphere here was dry and fresh, and the broad-leaved palms along the streets looked vigorous and gay. The train had stopped in a main thoroughfare. On the pavements, up and down the low line of shops, a brightly-coloured and coolly-dressed stream of white and coloured folk strolled along. Through a broad plate-glass shop-window I could see a dozen big, heavily-built white men being shaved. A few others were waiting in a row. Half a dozen negro lads were busily shining their shoes. Next door was the "pool" room, or billiards saloon. The open doors let you look into a shadowy, untidy-looking room. Half a dozen unkempt white men guffawed and joked as, shirt-sleeved and cigar-smoking, they drove seedy-looking snooker balls along the mottled green baize tables. Small, ragged-looking negro urchins picked the balls from the pockets and re-framed them for the break. Older ones marked up the score with long, graceful arms, gazing with resigned and untruculent boredom at the recreation of the superior race.

The only solid buildings in the town seemed a vermilion-red brick municipal hall and a couple of churches built in what looked like rough-cast. The shops seemed to be selling three things: huge golden pyramids of oranges, case after case of reddish-brown Coca-cola, and suits and shirts of white cotton or fawn gaberdine. The merchandise faithfully mirrored the sun. The panamas, the red bands on yellow straw, the pink ribbons on white linen dresses, the dust and the long, lazy gait of the man on the street also spoke of the climate. In the South, even at Christmas, they look out on life from under a broad and shady brim.

That afternoon one of the boys from the university drove me round the town. "Anything else you'd like to see," he said, as we dawdled along back into town from our visit to the great long belts of orange groves.

"Have you got a negro quarter?"

"Sure. I'll drive you through. But don't hold it against us."

We drove on into town, across the square, and past the municipal hall. A few hundred yards up the main road out, we turned to the left. At once we were in another town. Here the houses were dilapidated and shabby, the road uneven and gravelly, and the sidewalk, where there was one, pitted and crumbly. Some of the inhabitants sat on their steps or on the little verandahs. One man was pulling a half-rotted piece of planking from the floor of his verandah. Here and there windows were in need of glazing; every door was in need of a coat of paint. Though each house had a plot around it, there was no pretence to cultivation, let alone gardening. Weeds, broken boxes, and an occasional scrap of rusted iron were the only crop.

"Not too good, eh?" said my pilot. "But I give you my word, they get a better deal in this town than they do in many."

"Well, I don't know," I said, "but I should have thought that a drum of paint, a cartful of timber and a few yards of glass would give them a much better deal. And wouldn't cost much either."

"Yes," he said, steering the car past two children playing in the road with one hand, while he scratched his head with the other. "The only thing is, it won't do to brighten up the outsides of the houses, will it?"

"It'd be a start," I said.

"Don't know that it would even be a start," he said. "To do things for some of these people as they are now'd do more harm than good. They'd not know how to value good treatment. They'd think it was being soft. In any case, some of the white folks wouldn't stand for it. They reckon the negroes are getting too sassy anyway, nowadays."

Through the window I could see a group of big young negroes lounging at one of the street corners. They were strong, tough, brutish, their great, loosely-hanging limbs relaxed, their massive hands in their pockets, leaning back against the peeling woodwork of the saloon. They were eyeing a flashily-dressed young negress walking down the other side of the road. A burst of loud, coarse, almost animal laughter rose from the group. As we passed I saw their open mouths. The gums were thick and red, the white teeth even in mirth flashing savagely. The laughter gurgled up again from their throats, and as the car turned the corner I saw again the broad grinning mouths and the rolling whites of their eyes.

That evening I spent with Jesse Fagan, the town's leading doctor. He and his wife lived in a bungalow type of house, one big room with two bed-rooms, small dining-room and a bright, hygienic kitchen all leading off it.

"How d'you like my house?"

"Jolly nice. And very convenient."

"Any like these in England?"

"Jesse, don't be a fool," said his wife. "How d'you expect them to have houses like this in that climate."

He got to talking about the negroes. "Snag is," said Jesse, "that the poorest and most backward area economically, the South, has to carry a third of the negro population, and nearly two million poor whites as well. When folks comes here from New York and complain about our negro quarter, I say to them: 'You go up to

Chicago and see how they live there, where there's much more money, and better prospects economically. You'll see we don't do so badly for them down here.'"

"What do they say to that?"

"They point out that up there the negroes get more freedom than we give 'm here. 'True,' I say, 'but what do you want us to do? Let them do just what they please as from nine a.m. to-morrow morning?' No, sir. You can't start treating negroes like responsible grown-ups till you've given them the means of acting like that. It's a slow business that. It means more and more educational and health services; it means raising their standard of living. That means finding work for them which'll bring them in enough money to live like white men. And that's all worked in with the economic policy of the country as a whole, and God knows when we're going to start on that."

"How do they stand with the unions?" I asked.

"If you put up the negro's wages, or let him have completely free access to employment, a lot of the whites would complain. You'd think to read the papers sometimes that only the employers keep the negro down. No, often it's the white workers who want the negro kept right where he is, so's their own job's safe."

Outside, by the back door leading into the kitchen, I could see Helen, the big, fat, smiling negress cook. Her dark cocoa-coloured skin gleamed below the line of her yellow turban. She was peeling oranges into a big blue china bowl. She was humming a song about "The Lawd" and Moses.

"She seems happy enough," I said.

"Yes. She is. But what happens to the rest who don't belong to a good white home; and what we goin' to do with those who aren't so homey as Helen?"

"Are there any things you'd like to see done right away,

things that you think might get done if people really thought hard, and cared, about the problem?"

"Yes. Three things. First, I'd like to see the Federal Bill against lynching passed."

"I thought it *had* been passed."

"No, the House of Representatives have passed it several times, but the Senate's always failed."

"You know, people over here seem so sympathetic and naturally kind, I can't imagine how they're willing to *let* the Senate do that."

"Well, you know how these things are. They don't all keep up with the news, and they don't all read the records. In any case, the Senate as a whole don't just say 'No' to the bill; some guy gets up and proves that the thing is in some way taking away State Rights, or damaging them by Federal invasion, or something like that. You know how goddam jealous every state is of the Federal Government? Of course, this all happens *before* the bill gets to the voting stage."

"What're the other two things?"

"I'd like to see a Fair Employment Practices Act to give real good protection to the negroes against discrimination and ill-treatment by employers. And I'd like to see the poll tax abolished."

"What's the poll tax for?"

"'Tisn't what it's for so much as what it does. Certain states, seven of them down here and abouts, impose a poll tax which you've got to pay if you want to have the right to vote. Well, what with one legal racket and another, if they want to they can make it just too high to let a negro—or a poor white share-cropper—vote. Has some mighty funny results in a so-called democratic community. F'r instance in one of our neighbouring states, out of a million and a quarter people of voting age only about 200,000 qualified last time to go to the poll.

Only one man in six exercised the first democratic right. I'll bet Stalin had a good laugh at that."

Mrs. Fagan came back into the room. "You still talking like a Yankee radical?" she said. "Don't you let him talk you round, Mr. Harris. He starts off on the negroes, and then he gets round to politics. I know him. He cheats."

"Elsie," said her husband. "You're a very good woman. But you're a stubborn one. Talking about the negroes and about political and economic affairs goes together."

"Wanting to build houses like this in London," said Mrs. Fagan. "Mr. Harris, if that just doesn't show you how practical my husband is, I don't know what does. Come on in here, and have some southern fried chicken."

The chicken was good. Crisp, curly, and rich with fat.

About ten o'clock I started to walk back to my hotel. A few yards on, a taxi came round a corner slowly. I waved and it stopped. Opening the door, I saw there was a girl sitting in the back. "That's all right," said the driver. "Young lady lives my way. I'm giving her a lift home."

As we drove to my hotel they continued their drawling conversation as if I had not been there. " . . . So Ah told him," said the girl, "Ah know things are diffr'ent up here than they are daown Saowth. But Ah kin't get used to meetin' your negro friends so soon. Ah'm jist not used to it."

"What he say to that, Lu?"

"Oh, he was O.K. about it. But Ah got to make him see how we feel about it daown here. He ain't been in the Saowth. If he comes home with me, my folks'll get sore if he talks about negroes the way he does up theyur."

"Sure. Whaddya going to do?"

"Ah really don't know, Bill. Ah don't know whether

Ah ought to go on seein' him or not. And that's the truth. Ah don't know if a marriage could git along with two people having such different 'pinions on the coloured folks, do you?"

"I sure don't know, Lu."

And America doesn't know either.

Two days later, at the Gideonville railroad station, I stood and watched the coloured folk walking out from the "coloured" entrance, about thirty yards up the platform. A negro carrying a pig-skin suitcase and champagne-coloured gloves crossed to drink from the water-tap marked "Coloured" and a negress bought her little boy some chocolate at a "coloured" store. As on nearly every railway station I saw, the porters, the famous "red-caps," were negroes. Some were nearly white, others coal-black. Some of the almost white-skinned had ugly, coarse, broad features; some of the almost black were lean and refined.

The train carried us through typical deep south countryside. There was damp, sandy soil, and often the track was bordered by a tall reedy-looking plant whose thin leaves buckled in the wind like a giant kind of grass. Sometimes we looked out on where the sugar-cane grew. A line of negroes bent under the bundles on their backs. Further on, a knot of brightly- but raggedly-dressed pickers, resting from the fields, ate their food huddled in the shelter of a wooden hut.

"Haow d'you like the Saowth," asked the big, burly man opposite me.

"It's fascinating," I said. "To an Englishman, anyway."

"What strikes you most about it?"

"The colour."

"Which kind of colour. Local or racial?"

"Both."

"Uh-huh."

We both went on looking out of the window again. Then, "By the way," I said. "How many negroes are there in the United States?"

"Over thirteen million, I guess. I read somewhere last week that one American citizen in ten is black. Waal, black or mulatto."

"What's a mulatto?"

"Part black, part white. Lot of states got laws against intermarriage, and against . . . you know what. And it just shows what a law-abiding and well-behaved country we are: we got six million mulattoes."

"Is that so?" I said.

"It certainly is." The man opposite leaned forward with an obvious desire to add a good deal more. "The whole thing is this way——" he said. But the train was rapidly slowing down.

"This is where I get out," I said. "Thanks for the talk."

"That's O.K.," he said.

When I landed on the platform I found that he had his head out of the window. "Say," he said, smiling, "I guess you've heard a hundred times that you can't understand the negro problem unless you've lived inside it, huh?"

"Yes," I said. "Hundreds of times."

"Well," he said. "It's still true. Have a good trip."

CHAPTER XV

Americans in Hollywood

AT seven in the morning the tarmac on the Montana airfield was a couple of inches in snow. On the hills to the north the trees were thick with it, and the wind blew bitterly from the east. Inside the twin-engined Douglas the warmth sent us all to sleep. Once, for a few moments at noon, I awoke to gaze down on the purple crags and ochreous screes of Nevada. Then, at four o'clock, I awoke again. Below us lay the red roofs and square white buildings of Sacramento. Ahead lay the blue waters of San Francisco Bay, the towns of Richmond to the north and Oakland to the south. The great white bridge soared in its graceful span, eight miles across the bay, to where San Francisco itself lay upon the lower of the two mountain walls which make the glorious Golden Gate. Before us and below, dead in line with our line of flight, the setting sun had laid a bar of flame upon the water. The shimmering band receded from us, narrowing as it passed out through the mountain walls, rising into the dim, unhorizoned Pacific, up through the misty glow to meet the reddening orb. The picture changed in colour and harmony as the sun fell and we moved nearer. The blue of the sea in the distance, the white and red roofs twinkling on the purple hills, the deep shadows and the olive-green trees—there could be nothing like them in England. The air was so clear and the sky so pure, every line stood out as though a pen had etched it. "California the Golden" is what they call it. And certainly, if you first come upon it by air it is easy to believe that this is the most blessed and bountiful and brightly-coloured region of the earth.

When in the same day a man has worn overcoat and muffler for breakfast, and for his supper sits out of doors in an open-necked shirt, he begins to ponder on how much climate influences the way he thinks and what he thinks about. Life was much simpler and easier from the material point of view at that supper-table than it had been at breakfast. How different were the ratios of time spent on wondering how to keep warm. How much better one's temper was. How much more amiable one's fellow creatures seemed to be. Even the local inhabitants for whom the novelty must have worn off—though novelty in California is a local industry—seemed to take life in a more philosophic and easygoing fashion. Their hair seemed smoother, and neater, in a natural, not an artificial, way. There was no wind, and there was no need for them to be always putting on or taking off their hats. Their collars were cleaner and less crumpled: of course—they were not always pulling off scarves or struggling into overcoats. Their voices had none of the windy, nasal twang of the east, nor the gruff tones of the mid-west. The Californian tan on their faces—something between an Anglo-Saxon pink and a tropical bronze—made them look quietly, not too heartily, healthy.

From San Francisco we flew down to the huge sprawling city of Los Angeles. As one goes up and down its vast frame of boulevards, one senses from time to time, as gradually shops and cinemas become more dense, that one is coming upon some square, or circle, or other kind of town centre. At that very moment the houses and shops begin rapidly to thin out again. "Ah, well," you say. "It's nice to get back in the country again." At that moment you strike three or four churches and a fire station and, in a second or two, are back in a road as busy as Oxford Street. The city has no centre for its three million inhabitants. It has as much character as a big grid of Slough High Streets.

Back in New York I had met Arthur Hornblow, MGM producer. "You're coming to Los Angeles?" he said.

"Yes," I said.

"Well," he said. "I expect you'll be pretty busy. But if you care to look at a studio or two and have a meal you might drop me a card."

"All right, I will," I said.

"That's if you're not too tired and busy," he said.

"Oh, yes," I said. "Quite." Tired and busy! We'd have taken that invitation if we'd taken it in invalid chairs.

At intervals during the next eight weeks my colleagues asked me if I had let Arthur Hornblow know precisely when we would arrive in Los Angeles.

"Now, look here," I would say. "These big-shot producers are very busy men. Perhaps he's forgotten."

"Did he, or did he not, tell you to drop him a card?"

"He did."

"Well, why the hell don't you write?"

I wrote.

Within a few hours of reaching Los Angeles we were debating. After it the debaters took us to a party. It took place in a street of the oddest houses I have ever seen. Any one of them would have made a street look bizarre; this street had three hundred of them in it. Each was different: Moorish, Scandinavian, Spanish, Peruvian, Mexican, Victorian and perpendicular Gothic, every style—pure or bastard—had reproduced itself along the trimly-turfed and tree-planted banks of that two-mile boulevard. The house at which we stopped was finished in rough-cast. On the windows were crusty, clay-coloured embattlements, and here and there a stuccoed turret. It was divided into two flats. We went to the higher one, climbing up to it from the front lawn by a twisting, medieval staircase.

Inside we found attractively rococo, but very comfortable furniture. The owner was quite a remarkable young woman. Tiny, jet-haired, sloe-eyed and volatile, she was, among other things, the West Coast Debating Champion for 1945. On the mantelpiece of one of the rooms were arranged her trophies—little models of orators in action, fashioned in silver and set on ebony blocks. Some figures had their hands raised in beseeching gestures, others pointed a finger to the skies. They were in lounge suits, not togas.

Our hostess was modest about herself, enthusiastic about us. "You were terrific, you boys," she said breathlessly. She spoke at a very fast pace, and threw her arms and hands up and down to show she meant what she said. "You were fantastic, terrific—have a drink—you were fabulous." We grinned sheepishly. None of us, we pointed out, were west coast champions. "And you looked so wonderful on that platform," she raced on. "So grotesque." We stiffened. "Your hair down flat, and so long. Your suits, your shoes—boys! you were fabulous."

"What do you mean, 'our suits'?" we said.

"Oh, your suits! Those funny little lapels. Those vests, your tight jackets, your *collars*!" She threw up her hands and dissolved in helpless laughter. The Oxford debaters smiled wanly.

It was a good party, and we liked the people we met. They were kind, as all Americans seemed to be, but in the matter of hospitality even deafer than most to the word "No." There was no talk about the film-world, but in the conversation there was a touch of the speed and pungency we hear on the screen—"I told that guy: 'Say,' I said. 'If you had brains, you'd be dangerous.'"

At about two in the morning we decided that we had better go home to our hotel. "I'll drive you," said the west coast champion.

"We can't let you do that. It's two o'clock."

"Aw, that's nothing. I got to go back to college to-night, anyway."

Next morning Arthur Hornblow rang up. "Try and get out here by ten," he said.

"Fine."

"Have you boys got a car?"

"No. I'm afraid——"

"I'll send one round."

We drove out about twenty miles to Culver City in a big, black, luxury saloon. Our driver pointed out the various studios as we passed them. "Only four left in Hollywood itself," he said. "Most of them're out in Culver City or here, in the San Fernando valley." We were skimming along through a long narrow pass with olive-green hills on either side, now steep, now rolling away gently. The broad white road was neat and trim as a length of felting. The precise shapes and clean bright colours of the buildings, their brown doors and their red roofs, gave them a stagey look. The sky was the same colour at the horizon as it was above our heads, a mat blue. The sun shone with light that was brilliant but not fierce. Everything seemed artificial, perfect and controlled. You felt that at any moment a film-director would shout "Cut!" and the scene be deluged in darkness.

Arthur Hornblow sat in a comfortable, richly-furnished room which was a cross between an office and a study. On the walls were some handsome photographs. There were interesting magazines and art books on the small table in front of me, and quaint pieces of wood-carving on the walls. "I've got somebody to take you round this morning," he said. "We're making two pictures just now. When you've seen all you want to, he'll bring you back here, and we'll go out for some lunch. If that's all right with you."

"That'll be all right," we said.

Leaving the huge white administrative block, which looked like a municipal hall, we walked across to the sets. Big hangar-like sheds stood among smaller and lower buildings so that the place looked rather like an aerodrome. "In here," said our guide.

The studio was a very large one. Its stone walls, the corrugated iron roof with metal girders, suggested a drill hall. We threaded our way between bits of photographic apparatus, furniture and pieces of scenery to where a big mechanism looking rather like a highly-japanned, streamlined crane was standing. It was the camera. About fifteen yards in front of it was erected something between the stage of a small-town variety theatre and the kind of platform on which young ladies pose outside the booths at fairs and circuses. On each side of the camera were massed huge floodlights. More hung down from the roof, and there were batteries housed in boxes and balconies halfway up the walls. When the lights were full on, everything and everybody glowed faintly, as plums and peaches glow with the blue morning bloom. On the stage stood ten young men and women. Their faces were hard and heavy with clay-coloured paints and purple rouge, their dance costumes a mass of solid blues, reds and yellows. The background behind them was equally crude and bright. "We're shooting this in Technicolor," said the guide.

Near the camera was a ladder ten feet high. On the top sat a plump-faced, grey-haired man. He wore a dark-brown soft cloth suit and leather slippers. In his hand he held a small microphone. His quiet, friendly voice was relayed all round us. He was explaining that he wanted a shot of the curtains coming across the stage at the end of the dance. "Give me that," he said, "and we'll break for lunch. O.K.?"

"O.K."

"Quiet please, then."

From somewhere on the stage a man looking rather like Fred Astaire appeared. He wore a white flannel suit, "co-respondent's shoes," a straw hat with a red band, and a malacca cane. He stood in front of the camera while a boy came up and held a piece of board in front of him. Both disappeared. Then the real Fred Astaire came on and stood, in his flannel suit and red-banded straw hat, exactly where his double had been.

"Music," said the director.

"We've recorded that separately," whispered our guide. At that moment a wild and syncopated orchestral blast roared out from behind the stage. The ten members of the chorus and Fred Astaire limbered up, executing a few movements in their own time to get paced up to the music.

"Camera," said the director softly.

At that instant, chorus and Fred Astaire leaped, hell for leather, into the full rhythm of the dance. The camera on the beam of the crane rolled forward, poised for a few seconds before the face of Fred Astaire, rose slowly to six feet above his head, and then, suddenly, fell away, downwards and backwards, in a swooning, swan-like curve. Slowly the curtains came across until the broadly-smiling famous face of Fred Astaire was shut out. It all happened in about ten seconds.

"Not quite," said the director. He looked up at the camera-man on the beam. "How was that for you, Tommy?"

"The curtains came too fast," said Tommy.

"Thought so. We'll try it again."

Up on the stage, Fred Astaire was having the sweat soaked up from his face and temples by a man with a handkerchief. Somebody else was holding his hat, gloves and stick. The ten men and girls breathed heavily, and relaxed in any kind of posture the stage had room for.

"O.K., Fred?" said the director.

"O.K., Johnnie."

"O.K., girls?"

"O.K."

Once again the music rushed out on us in full swing and mid-bar. There was something frightening about its sudden, unheralded diapason. Once again, Fred Astaire moved slightly to the music, swayed and curvetted and then, at the appointed second, leaped into a dervish-like series of steps, swings and whirls. Once again the curtains came across.

"How was that, Tommy?"

"Curtains bit too slow."

As soon as the music had stopped, the girls had dropped their smiles and relaxed their limbs again. They seemed to get an extra degree of rest out of being ungainly, leaning awkwardly against a property balustrade, or squatting on a step, with their knees apart and their beautiful shoulders hunched. They looked like one of Degas's paintings of the ballet girls. Fred Astaire's sweat honoured another handkerchief.

"Have to try this again, girls. O.K., Fred?"

"O.K.," said Fred Astaire. He looked hot but not bothered. In between shots he chatted with the chorus or talked to Tommy up on the beam. Apart from the heat he seemed to enjoy it all.

"Quiet, please."

The music roared. The actors danced as furiously as

ever. The camera swooned deliciously and Fred Astaire's smile was broad and bright as the curtains closed.

"Perfect," said the director. He took a comb from his pocket and patted his fine silvering hair down behind his ears. "That all right for you, Tommy?"

"Fine," said Tommy.

"Nice work, girls," said the director. "That'll do for the morning."

We walked out into the sunlight which seemed no brighter, and certainly less warmer, than the studio atmosphere. "That was a pretty tough take you saw," said our guide. "It's hard if you're making a picture with dancing in it. Those girls have been doing the kind of thing you saw since about nine this morning. They had to be here by seven to get made-up." A few of them went by us on their way to the dressing-rooms. They were chattering as brightly as sparrows, but they looked tired under the paint.

"Did you notice how quickly the main lights were dimmed when there was a hold-up for a second or two?" went on our guide. "Making moving pictures is so expensive no economy's too small to be worth while. You can't afford to waste a second of your power—it's one of the most expensive items. By the way, I expect Mr. Hornblow told you that if there's anything you want to know about anything, just ask. We've got no secrets here."

We entered a much smaller studio. It was quite dark, except for a glow at the far end where a much smaller camera and lighting set was arranged round a court scene. As we walked over carefully in the shadows, the rich plummy voice of Edward Arnold floated over. "Do you really love her, little girl?" he said. He was the judge. "Yes, I do, I do," came the tense little voice of Margaret O'Brien.

"Cut," said the director. People began to breathe again and to move about. We could not hear what the director was saying, but we could hear the tones of his voice as he spoke to Margaret O'Brien. He seemed to be telling her what she was supposed to be thinking and feeling in the next few feet of film. His even, polite, persuasive voice had a hypnotic quality. "Yes, all right," we heard her say. She gave him a sweet, very child-like smile.

"She's a grand kid," said our guide. "But she's an awful worry to have on the set."

"Why's that?"

"She's of compulsory school age. She's got to have four hours' schooling a day, before the hour of four o'clock. Otherwise we'd get prosecuted by the Federal Government. We have to keep a governess on the spot to fit the lessons in—that's her over there with the stop-watch. If they can't be fitted in between the kid's shots the whole production's got to take time off while she sits down and draws a few cows or does some fractions. That kid's education is the most expensive in the United States. And, boy, don't this company know it."

Outside again, we visited some of the outdoor sets. We saw the artificial canal on which still stood the barge on which *Tugboat Annie* was made. We walked down Cornish quays into Piccadilly, and turning first left came into Times Square, New York. Further on was a large tank of water. "The effects men are having lunch," said our guide, "or I'd ask them to fix you a storm."

Edward Boyle caught sight of a wallmap which listed the main outdoor sets. "You've got 'Eton College' here," he said. "Could we see it?"

"I'm sorry, Sir Edward," said the guide, "but the place has gone to pieces."

Over in the Warner Brothers studios we were taken

to see a lavish production called *Don Juan.* It was being made on the biggest indoor set in Hollywood, and every inch was being used for the court scenes. On the shining, black, polished floors stood knots of lovely women in low-bodiced silken gowns, and elegant, bearded grandees. Men in blue overalls and rope-soled shoes were moving carefully between them, sweeping away dust and particles of thread. At the edge of the black floor the Spanish queen was resting. Her dress was so elaborate that she could not sit down in it. She reclined against a long, rubber-faced plank, and propped her elbows on arms four feet from the ground. She was a Swedish beauty comparatively new to Hollywood.

When we first saw her she was reading the *Reader's Digest.* Her deep-blue eyes gazed out frankly and kindly at us, but looked a little tired. Her hair was glossy, almost greenish, like the raven's black. It had been dyed. Her own was golden.

"Which colour do you prefer?"

"I don't know," she said, in a slow solemn voice. "But I was very hurt when I found that my two children hadn't noticed that it had been done."

The Duke de Lorca came up. "I hear you're not doing too badly in the debates," he said. His dark eyes and swarthy beard made him look a perfect Spaniard, but he was an Englishman, Robert Douglas. "I wish I were more happy about this government," he said. "Look what they're doing about requisitioning houses. My brother——" We got into a long, four-cornered discussion on emergency powers and nationalization.

"Duke de Lorca!" shouted somebody.

"That's me," he said. "They're shooting me on the main staircase. Very painful it is too."

We said good-bye to the beautiful Swedish Queen of Spain and passed out into the sunlight. We followed the clean white road till we came to another door with red lights winking above it. "Bette Davis is making a picture in here," said our guide. "I'll just see if she minds you coming in. Sometimes she doesn't like strangers on the set." He went in. In a second or two he was out again. "O.K.," he said.

The studio was another big one, but except for some dressing-rooms near the door it was empty-looking. At the far end a group of men in shirt-sleeves were standing around the open end of a U-shaped canvas and three-ply screen. We walked over and found that inside the screen was a small set representing one side of a sitting-room. There were some chairs, a book-case, ornaments and a fireplace. On the nearside of the fireplace, with its back to the camera, was a leather-backed armchair. I counted up the number of men standing by. There were twenty-eight.

"What are they all for?"

"Everybody belongs to a union. Union of carpenters, union of hair-dressers, and so on. The unions won't let any job be done by a man who isn't doing that job for a living. If you want a wisp of hair put back on the actor's forehead, you've got to send for the hair-dresser. So, in case anything happens, you've got to have the whole bunch standing by."

Some of the men were sitting down in property chairs talking in low tones, some were tinkering with lights, switching bulbs on and off. A small group stood in one corner and discussed an accident which had happened to "Louis." "You could have slid him in under the door," said one.

"All right," said an authoritative voice suddenly. "Let's take it."

A young woman flew by us and disappeared into the dressing-rooms. Men started to clear off the little set and range themselves behind the camera. Behind me I heard a swish of skirts. I turned and saw Bette Davis striding along in our direction. In her tight-waisted, long black skirt, and closely-fitting, black, woollen jumper, the elegance of her figure was striking. She moved with a swift, imperious gait, her arms swinging lightly from the shoulder. Her hair was combed down tightly and shone like a light-coloured gold. Her wide eyes were deep china-blue. They had an electric flash in them which the screen cannot give.

The director had a word with her. She listened to him with a polite, composed, slightly suffering kind of attention. Then the action began. It consisted of her moving from the centre of the room, picking up a shawl, taking it to the chair in which a man was sitting, being about to put it on his knees, getting gently exasperated with him, and dropping it on his knees with a "Do-it-yourself-then" kind of look. There was no sound, and no word. The cameras rolled for about ten seconds. Miss Davis did the shot six times. To the onlooker it seemed the same each time, but after the sixth somebody gave a grunt and the twenty-eight men sighed with relief.

At twelve-thirty we climbed into Arthur Hornblow's shining Cadillac. We purred our way over undulating roads under the hot sun to Beverly Hills. The broad streets were lined with tall, broad-leaved palms. "Well," he said. "What d'you think of the studios?"

"A lot quieter and more businesslike than we expected."

"It's usually like that," he said. "People come here expecting to find something between a night-club and a circus, and find a hard-working factory."

"The directors seemed so matter-of-fact."

"Yes. Now and again somebody comes over here with

a fine big Central European temperament. But as soon as they show it, they get the bird, and they either shut up or disappear."

"How do the actors and actresses really live here?"

"Well, you know what so-called artistic people can be like. But you've got to remember that making motion pictures is a tough job. You don't feel like raising hell every night if you've to be on the set from eight to five. Most people here enjoy home like everybody else, and want to get back to it when they get a chance. Mind you," he added, "a lot of them have tried a few different homes."

"Why do we hear so much about Hollywood night life and eccentricities?"

A few boys and girls play around, and the gossip writers and publicity men fan the stuff out all over the world. You know how it is. Considering how exacting the film-world is, it's extremely balanced. Then, quite apart from the films, California's always been a favourite place with cranks, revolutionaries, and religious maniacs. On top of that, there's a lot of industrial money in the state—oil and aircraft. Rich people come out here and combine business with pleasure. They can get both, hot and heavy, around here."

We lunched at Romanoff's. "Supposed to be one of the three best restaurants in the world," said our host. As we entered, the proprietor, Prince Romanoff, came up. We were introduced to him. "What colleges in Oxford?" he asked.

"New College, Wadham and Christ Church."

"I was at Magdalen," he said. He went off murmuring something about getting a lunch which one Oxford man could decently put in front of another.

"Is he related to the Romanoff's who used to rule in Russia?"

"So he claims. But he doesn't speak to them now. And he says they spell their name with a 'v'."

We sat down and ate tiny Olympia oysters, some salmon, and a minute steak. The cooking was far too good for young men, but we didn't allow the quality to put us off. We began to talk about the Hollywood trials. "Crazy," said Hornblow. "They just don't know where they are. All over the shop. People talk about 'our radicals' over here. Our radicals couldn't even get into your Tory party. But the trouble is only one man in a thousand over here knows it."

Though he had only lived in England a couple of years, Hornblow liked the country. "My father was born there," he said. "He was always set on going back, and when he retired from films, he went. He took a house in Hampstead and bored himself to death." The talk got around to the Grand Canyon. "You mustn't miss that," he said. "Get there at dawn or sunset and watch the changes in the light on the different layers of rock. It'll make a geologist out of you on the spot." One of us said that he'd heard the human race could be packed into a box, and that the box could lie unnoticed at the bottom of the Canyon. Hornblow stopped chewing for a moment. "That's not a bad idea," he said.

During and after the meal he introduced us to a number of people. Sir Cedric Hardwicke was sitting near the door looking magnificently English. "These boys have beaten the best debaters in the States," said Hornblow. Sir Cedric's left eyebrow lifted slightly. "Of course," he murmured. For a moment we talked to Charles Boyer. Charm, courtesy and intelligence radiated from him like rays from the sun. Looking back on it, I realized he was somewhat bald. At the time, his face and his voice monopolized the attention.

As we were going off, Hornblow said. "You boys

oughtn't to waste the whole of your holiday around the studios. There are lots of interesting things to see—the mountains at Pasadena, the coast at Santa Barbara. You should go and see the Huntington Library and the Art Gallery. I'll ring up and fix the tickets. And you might go——"

"How far away's Santa Barbara for instance?"

"Eighty miles."

"I don't see how we can get out so far. We're only here three days more, and the trains——"

"Forget about the trains. That Cadillac you had this morning, and the man that's driving, is yours so long as you're in Hollywood. Just send him home when you've finished in the evenings. Otherwise he'll stay outside and wait."

We began to mumble thanks, but Hornblow cut us short. "That's all right," he said. "I owe England a lot she never asks me for."

We used the car to cover a couple of hundred miles of California country. We saw the collection of eighteenth-century paintings at the Huntington, and the great white colonnaded gallery. We saw Gainsborough's "Blue Boy," and a fine collection of original manuscripts. The institution was created by a benefactor who made his millions in the chancey, rough-and-tumble days of the early railways. Some Americans we heard talk of him as a man who shows what cultured heights the rugged individualist can rise to. Others said that this is just another case of how the heritage of American citizens is plundered by robbers who seek to sanctify their crimes by paying blood-money to the Fine Arts.

One day we drove up on to the purple peak of Mount Wilson. There, through the opening of its round white house, the great one hundred-inch telescope looked out to the heavens. From the observation perch which jutted out above the steeply-descending valley, we watched the swiftest and most colourful sunset I have ever seen. Then we raced back down the dusky sides of the mountains in the great black car, the cleverly-constructed road taking us down so quickly that my ears pained me as they did when coming down from the skies in an aeroplane. Cars around these parts are fitted with altimeters as well as speedometers.

That night we stood in the Hollywood Boulevard to watch the first of the series of grand parades which take place nightly for a month before Christmas. Thousands of people were thronging the long broad streets. Big imitation Christmas-trees stood in illuminated tubs. Spangled and tinselled streamers hung like silken bridges across the highway. Everywhere there was light, colour and sparkle. Music, laughter, and the popping of fire-crackers besieged the ear. The procession took two hours to pass. Band after band went by, squadron after squadron of cowboys on light-brown, almost pink, horses with long, flowing tails and manes. A troop of red-coated pseudo-Canadian mounties trotted past, a fake Highland Regiment with skirling pipes and swinging kilts, a pipe-clayed theatrical band of American marines. The crowd roared with joy as their favourite Wild West film star pranced by on a milk-white mustang with a pink muzzle. They laughed or booed as a very real chief of police, or mayor, or district attorney trundled slowly by in a car bearing his name and office.

The great glamorous stars of international fame were studded at intervals along this rout of colour and romance. Some were on their own, some in couples or a small group, standing or sitting on chariots and ornamented trucks, the women often sealed off from the evening breeze in diaphanous nylon or cellophane domes. Glorious, tumbling, chestnut hair, flashing smiles and silk-distending curves took each male eye. Women film-fans gazed at the broad shoulders and majestic or impudent glances of their favourite masculine type. Each star seemed to appear not in his or her own right, but in association with some firm's soap or tooth-paste, shampoo or body-unguent. The crowd screamed or sighed its varying moods of adulation, but kept an eye on the advertisements. It was as though the gods had come down from Olympus to visit the faithful earthlings, but had come with practical advice on how to look and smell, if not to be, like them.

While the procession was on, the traffic was paralysed for five square miles. For two hours every night till Xmas, the hard-working, hard-playing, quick-witted city of oil, air and celluloid was to become a mass of wide-eyed, clapping, grown-up children.

We left Hollywood with regret. Everyone there had been kind, human and amusing. The food had been good, the beds comfortable, and everybody very pleasant. Nobody seemed to be suffering from the proximity of the world's forcing-house of make-believe. We were relieved to find far less skin-deep beauty and much more common-sense than most British writers on the subject had led us to expect.

CHAPTER XVI

Americans and "You British"

THE big American sitting in the next chair of the Pullman smoking-car put down his paper and turned to me.

"You bin laughing there for ten minutes," he said. "What's biting yuh?"

"It's this book. It's so damn funny."

He looked at me hard when he heard my accent. "You're English?"

"That's right."

"Say, I didn't think you Limies *could* laugh."

"If all the stories in this book are as good as this one," I said, "I'll laugh everybody out of this Pullman before we get to Missoula."

"Say, what *is* that book, anyway?"

"*My Life and Hard Times*, by James Thurber."

His eyes widened. "But that's an *American* book!"

"That's right."

"Well, darn it. I didn't think an Englishman would laugh at American humour."

I was getting the lingo. "You just stick around," I said.

He turned back to his paper with a mystified air. I went on with my laughing. In a few minutes he went out, shaking his head. Later, while I was turning over a page, I heard his voice outside in the corridor. "Yeah," he was saying. ". . . and he says he's English."

Jokes about nationalities often show what one country thinks about another. At a debate on the west coast we heard one of the more chestnutty jokes about the English. A big, red-faced American debater had strolled over to the rostrum. He beamed down at the audience. "Before I begin," he said, "I want to tell you a li'l story." (This was rather unorthodox for the opening of an American debate, but this young man was the All-American Impromptu-Speech champion for 1947, and consequently was expected to go off his script a bit.) "The last Englishman who came here, ladies 'n gen'l'men . . ." He went on to say that the Englishman was told a well-known American funny story in which the last word, and the key-word, was "spittoon." "Haw-haw-haw," said the Englishman. "Very funny, old boy. Jolly good joke, old man. Gad, sir, I must tell that to my friends." Later, the Englishman tells the joke to his friends, but when he comes to the last word he says "cuspidor" instead of "spittoon." He laughs very heartily, and cannot understand why his friends do not.

"Which reminds me of another," said the champion, beaming more broadly than before, and obviously rather proud of the way he pronounced "Bai Jove!" "And this story, ladies 'n gen'l'men, may explain why the British post-war recovery is so slow, *even* with Nationalization." He turned and gave us a grin. "No offence, fellas. It seems, ladies 'n gen'l'men, that during the war, a plane was flying 'cross the Pacific. In this plane was a crew of eight, made up, by chance, of two Scots, two Jews, two Americans and two Englishmen. Waal, owing to engine trouble it had to land on a desert island. They had to spend a few weeks there, before a ship sighted them. When the rescue party put in they found that these couples had all been busy. The two Scots were distilling a kind of whisky out of palms, the two Jews were working a credit system outah coconuts, the two Americans were making a sky-scraper out of dried leaves and mud, and the two Englishmen—waal, you know, ladies and gen'l'men, the two Englishmen were waiting to be introdooced."

One of the difficulties the Britisher is up against when he travels in the U.S.A. is that it is his virtues which the Americans find most difficult to understand and value. The Britisher, for instance, admires modesty. Many Americans esteem it too, but the greatest single laugh I heard in the United States was against that British quality. It was in a Hollywood cinema. The film we were looking at was *The Secret Life of Walter Mitty*, with Danny Kaye playing the name part. In one episode he is a handsome British R.A.F. fighter ace. He walks into the aerodrome mess, fresh from his latest kill, detached, courteous, rather diffident, the personification of understatement. The air-commodore goes up to him. "Good show, Mitty, old man," he says, in a casual tone. "That makes your bag seventy-eight, doesn't it?"

"Er—no, sir," says Mitty, in a quiet, politely offhand tone. "Seventy-six, eckshually. Two are only probable."

If the Englishman's modesty is understood and appreciated by very many Americans, the same cannot be said for his reserve. "We never know whether the English are enjoying themselves or not," we heard hostesses say several times. "They're so quiet about it." In some places we found that the English had a reputation for being ungrateful. "Thenks awfully. Thenk you verrah much," mimicked one girl to us. "And they say it in such thin, piping voices," she added. "Why don't they say: 'Lady, that's reel beautiful of you'?"

Her remark made me think of some of the live English I had met on the tour: a beady-eyed little charge-hand from a Midlands cotton mill, sitting hunched and suspicious on the edge of a chair, his wife, black-dressed and reticent, near a green plant which her presence was beginning to make look like an aspidistra. A wispy-moustached man from Manchester, a little blear-eyed with a red nose. Small, reserved, calculating-looking and cagey, the American personalities around them made them seem thin and unhappy figures. Solid, rather loveable, and certainly typical characters in their own country, the simple outspoken American background reduced them to caricatures. Their reserve, the care with which they avoided personalities and answered direct questions in respectably hackneyed clichés, was as striking as the stiffness of the novelist's travelling public schoolman, as foreign as the two lately-landed Oxford men we met, all pose and not an ounce of poise. Outspoken Scots, bluff Yorkshiremen, the emotional and talkative Celt, the big West Countryman, these are the figures the Americans take to. Many of the rest of us go down as grinders of invisible axes, the more dangerous and sharp for not being seen.

"Yes," I said to one young Juno who was showing me how the American girl should be held while dancing. "On the whole, we're a shy race."

"But what've you got to be shy *about*?"

"We've just *got* that way."

"When I dance with an Englishman I've got to hang round his neck, or I'd get out of speaking distance to him."

"You ought to see the Englishman in the Hammersmith Palais de Danse."

"Palay de Dongse! That sounds more like it!"

A thoughtful young American male standing by, said: "There's a good deal to be said for the kind of shyness which makes American girls hang round your neck when you dance, anyway."

"Don't you think they should?" said my partner to him.

"Oh, sure I do. You don't have to push them from inertia like shunting a truck as you have to with the English girls." His face became even more thoughtful. "Still," he said, "English girls are fine when they've started."

The Englishman's reserve sometimes frightens Americans so much that they themselves become inhibited. This is saying something. After our first debate outside the New York area, the Professor of Speech came running on to the platform with outstretched hands. Before the debate he had seemed quiet and nervous. "You're human," he almost sobbed. "Gosh! I needn't have worried!"

"Worried?"

"Sure. I couldn't eat my dinner for wondering how you'd go down."

"Well, would it have mattered?"

"I've only just taken over the speech here. Booking you boys was my first kind of official piece of work. Some of the other folks here said the British wouldn't go down. Too frosty. But, gee, you were real warm!"

A female voice came from behind us. "I'll say they were. And I thought the British were cold-blooded." She was one of those sparkling boyish-looking mid-western co-eds which America seems to turn out almost as expertly and quickly as her automobiles—fair-haired, blue-eyed, bright green, new-look dress.

"How many Englishmen have you met?"

"Never even seen one till to-night."

"Well, what makes you think we're so cold-blooded?"

"Movies."

"Anything else you think about us because of the movies?"

"You're formal."

"What d'you mean, formal?"

"You kinda like to do things *right.* I guess you do 'em right, too, over there."

"Thanks very much. Er—what kind of things?"

"Oh, I don't know. Wearing the right clothes, having your servants very well trained, going to the right school and that kind of thing. You know what I mean?"

"Yes, I know what you mean."

"I suppose that's all wrong?"

"As near as makes no difference all wrong."

"I'm glad. Why's it all wrong?"

"Well, there are about thirty million people in Britain who don't have and haven't had any servants, haven't had any choice of a school, and precious little choice about clothes."

This conversation was, we found, a useful one to have had so early. From then on when asked by any reception committees if we would like to wear "tuxedo" for the debate, we did not take this as a courteous way of saying that they would like us to do so. We said straight out that we'd only wear the things if they particularly wanted them. And the answer nearly always was: "Gosh, no. We only suggested the darn things because we thought, being British, *you'd* want to!" The conversation also explained to us how, mysteriously, at Minneapolis, everybody on the night train knew two Englishmen had jumped aboard the train at the last moment. It was because we were still wearing our dinner jackets. "The British change for dinner, even when travelling by train," we heard.

With the Britisher's reputation for reserve goes his reputation for being "a diplomat," a word which seems to have about as unpleasantly ambiguous a meaning as "politician" did for Shakespeare. The British are considered to be well supplied with guile.

"I'm afraid we've got to go now," we'd say to our host at a party.

"Non—sense. You cain't go now. Why must you go, anyway?"

"It's getting rather late——"

"Oh, shucks. The pardy's just start'n up. Have 'nother li'l drink. Here y'are. Scotch. Help close th' dollar gap."

"Really, we must go. We've got to catch the six train to-morrow morning, and if we turn up at the next place tired it's not fair on them."

"Now, you British cain't fool *me*. *I* know what's cooking. There's 'another pardy."

"Really there's not."

"Oh, yes, there is. *Oh*, yes, there is. Don't pull that famous British d'plomacy here."

"Look here, honestly——"

"There you are, see?" says our swaying host, appealing to the beaming crowd. "Look at 'm blushing. Trying to make a sucker out 'f pore ole Yank. You British! Naughty. V'ry naughty. Uncle Sam spank."

Whether most Americans still believe that Woodrow Wilson and other American statesmen have been consistently hoodwinked by European diplomats, and whether this is attributed to our greater political experience or to sheer trickery, is not easy to say. Many of them are certainly dubious about the British diplomatic record, as much for its virtues as for its weaknesses. The famous *Chicago Tribune*, an extremely readable and interesting paper, was perhaps the greatest spreader we encountered of the anti-British bug; and it is on British diplomacy that its criticism seemed mostly to fasten. The anti-British sting of the paper, however, seemed rather neutralized by the antipathy it expresses to the industrial and financial east coast. In one editorial, for instance, the British Royal Family were accused in paragraph one of pushing the late Mr. Roosevelt into the war against

Japan; in paragraph two it said that he had personally arranged a war against Japan so that he could go down to history as a great militarist.

Some Americans told us that they thought a certain amount of jealousy underlay much American criticism of the British diplomacy. To-day, as America comes more and more into international affairs, she feels more and more her lack of a large, specially-trained and highly-qualified corps of permanent diplomats, and understands that to deal with such affairs on a large scale through rich amateurs and volunteer business men is not altogether practicable.

Many Americans, especially the more travelled and well-read, are very conscious of the patronizing attitude which many British people have adopted towards them in the past. "What should I read to know what books are being published in Britain?" asked a wealthy and cultivated American lady.

"I should read the ——" I said.

"Oh, I can't read *that*."

"Why not?"

"I can't stand the way they talk about American books."

"What's wrong with it?"

"Well, if an American book comes up for review they seem to assume that it's likely to be a bad one. If they find it's at all good they write about it as though they can't quite credit the fact. If it's a bad one they write with that awful British understatement, which makes you feel so small, hinting all the time that they're doing their best to be kind. And there's something worse than that."

"What could be worse than that?"

"If a piece of English scholarship comes up which is second-rate but not hopeless, they says it's 'very American.'"

Considering the long experience Americans claim to have had of being treated by visiting British as an inferior kind of Englishman, it is heartening to find how little pleasure they take in the temporary reversal of British fortunes. The comradeship of the war and memory of the gallantry which Churchill symbolizes for them, their genuine personal compassion, when they think of it, for suffering Europe—all these things outweigh any feeling there is in some places that the British are taking what was coming to them for a long time. In Chicago, where perhaps the taxi-cab driver and the girl in the drug-store were not quite as friendly to us as they would have been elsewhere, Wedgwood Benn walked up to a book store and bought a paper. "You British?" asked the woman behind the counter.

"That's right."

"Over here on a trip?"

"Debating tour."

The woman looked at him kindly. "Gosh," she said. "It must be nice for you boys to come to a country where the papers can say what they like." There was no gloating in her tone—she was pleased that we had got away for a bit. Anthony talked to her about the programme of the Socialist government.

"And they ain't all Reds?"

"I am happy to say, No."

"And they ain't gonna abolish the King?"

"That is not on the programme."

"Well, I guess we get things wrong here. Not that I'm one for kings, mind you. I reckon they don't suit over here."

In spite of their pride in being a republic, all the Americans we came in contact with seemed to be more interested in the doings of the Royal Family than most British people would be. To hear some of them talk you would think that they think that the average British householder spends a good deal of his or her spare time discussing the royalty in reverently-hushed voices. At "God Save the King," some of them thought an Englishman would spring to attention with loudly clicking heels and a tear in his eye. When, in answer to numerous questions about the broadcast of the royal wedding, we answered that we would not be getting up at four a.m. to hear it, some people thought it was because Wedgwood Benn was a "Labourite."

The Americans do not resent the Englishman's patriotism and his sentiment for the institutions of his country. On the contrary, they share them, and like to do for him what they would do for themselves. At several places we went to, the debate hall's Stars and Stripes was supplemented with a Union Jack. Once we visited a Kiwanis Club in a north-west town. It was a weekly luncheon meeting. As usual, the meeting began with the national anthem. While we all remained standing the chairman said: "To-day we have three young Britishers with us. Let us honour their great country by singing 'God Save the King.'" Republicans, Democrats, Liberals and anti-socialists, they rattled it off with a gusto that nearly took the roof off, each man singing for all he was worth, and looking straight at the faces of his British guests. We wondered how many British people could have done the same for American visitors.

There are dozens of other ideas which the Americans have about British, but nearly all of them stem from one rooted standpoint. For good or bad, the Americans think of us and see in us an old, historical country. They see us as heirs to all the good and bad things which tradition and a legacy from the past entails. They like us for it and sometimes they don't like us for it. "You're hide-bound," they say. Next moment, they say that they "envy us our atmosphere."

In the bus from Gainesville to Jacksonville in Florida I met a man who had been stationed during the war in Wiltshire.

"That's where I live," I said.

"Yuh do? Boy! Do I envy you! Which town?"

"The nearest is Melksham."

"Melksham. I used to march through that market place. Boy! What a wonderful place that was."

"Well, I don't think it's all that hot."

"But it's so *old*, so historical. Gosh! It was great. Them stone walls, so solid. So *old*."

"I don't want to disillusion you," I said. "But there's not a building there more than seventy-five years old!"

He turned round sharply and there was a touch of asperity in his tone. He looked at me with an expression which told me I didn't know when I was well off. "Compare it with *that*," he said, pointing from the window, at the dusty shack-bound highway of a passing town.

I heard the same kind of opinion from a boy who had just come back from Oxford.

"How did you like Oxford?"

"Swell. Best time I've ever had."

"What did you like about it?"

"Well, I liked having so much private instruction from a tutor instead of always being in class. And I liked the students. Underneath, they're more different than our boys are. But most of all I liked the place itself. It didn't look as if anybody had *built* it. It looked like it had *grown*."

It is only when the Englishman's attachment to the "Old Country" becomes obtrusive that the American is inclined to take umbrage about it. He may resent, for instance, the professor's wife who proclaims her British birth by a super Oxford accent, or by littering her drawing-room with piles of *Punch*, *The Tatler* and the *Illustrated London News*. "You know," said one American, "we get thousands of immigrants from Europe every year. They bring their music, their cooking, their legends, and even the smells of their old countries. But the only folks who're always *talking* about the country they came from are the English. Now why's that?"

"Because they're the only ones that came from a great country."

"Well, why didn't they stay there then?"

The behaviour of some English people in the U.S.A. is very puzzling to some of the natives. It can be embarrassing to the British visitor, just as the behaviour of some British visitors, being able to let their hair down socially for the first time in their repressed lives, is embarrassing to the British residents. English people we met at parties tended to converge on us and ask for news of the "Old Country." Some of their alarm about what that "awful government" was doing provoked the contempt even of reactionary American private enterprisers.

"If you're so worried, Jessie, why don't you git back there," said one man to his daughter-in-law. "These boys don't act like the place is going to the dogs!"

Others were inclined to be sentimental. "I must speak to you young men, before you go," said a middle-aged lady who had come to the States in 1939. "*Don't* go before I have a chance to talk to you about deah old England." An hour later we were about to sneak away. We were putting on our coats in the hall. There was a loud squawk from the dining-room. Out came our compatriot. "At last," she said. The whole of the dining-room listened. "Tell me," she said, standing with her hand at her throat. "Is everything all right?"

"Well, it's not *all* right, but we're getting along."

"Thank goodness," she sighed. A couple of dozen wide-eyed Americans gazed at us from the dining-room. "And Piccadillah," she said, blinking her eyes like a clockwork camera shutter. "Is deah Piccadillah still theah?"

My last evening in the U.S.A. I spent with Bob, a young man who had lived and studied in both countries and had worked during the war in the American State Department. I said something to him about the rise of Russia having made necessary a great change on American foreign policy.

"Russia's not the key to our foreign policy," he said. "It's Britain."

"I find that hard to believe, Bob," I said. "Surely what Americans feel towards Britain hasn't anything to do with her anxiety about Russia?"

"I think it has. Look at it this way. For years the American people have been conscious of this kind of screen of military and naval power, and of political stability, over there on the outer edge of Europe. They've known that it stood between them and—well, whatever might be on the other side. It was more than a screen, though. More than a thing. We got so many of our ideas, our political lessons, our tastes, and our models from there, it was like a person rather than a screen. A kind of father-figure, you might say. We used to complain, and criticise, and sulk, and snap our fingers, and show our muscles just like lots of guys do when they're growing up. But we knew the old boy was there, and if he was a bit of a nuisance when things were going easily, we knew he'd keep anybody from busting in and pinching our milk. Well, now we've got to look after ourselves."

"But you've already been doing it."

"With our fists. Now we've got to do a lot more thinking for ourselves too."

"Well, people here seem keen to do that."

"Sure they are. Growing guys always are. And it's nice to feel that you've got the business to yourself so young."

"What's the snag then?"

"Well, it's just that we've inherited it a little bit too soon. It's as if the old man got a heart-attack long time before the kid really expected it. He's mighty proud to be running things so soon, and he gets peevish when the old man starts criticising from the bed. But, also, he resents it that the old guy got knocked up so soon, and landed him in such a mess at such short notice. 'Why in hell d'you go and make out you weren't getting sick,' he says."

"Gosh," I said. "Some Americans I know would choke if you talked about Britain being your father!"

"Just a simple and possibly quite unreliable analogy I'm using. Forget it. Though, as a matter of fact, nearly every kid hates his father just for being his father at one time or another."

"You'd better say young person and old person. From our point of view, too. Britain's not as old as all that. Or as battered. We've just overworked ourselves recently, that's all."

"O.K. Have it your own way. The main thing to understand is that we're very ready to do our own share, but we don't quite know what it is. Remember, when we're running around here, a witch's broom for Reds in one hand, a sack of dollars for E.R.P. in the other, a musket on our shoulders and a darn great tin hat bouncing down on the bridge of our nose, we're also trying to get in a bit of schooling."

"Schooling?"

"Yes. Just two subjects. Majoring in "World Leadership." Minoring in "How to Grow Food." We're not aiming for honours—a pass'll do for us. You had about a century for that curriculum—and you certainly failed your minor. We've got a few years to succeed in both. If *we* fail, well, I guess there'll be a different school taking over; and the methods'll be different."

"Do you think Britain can help you learn quickly?"

"Sure. We're learning from you every day. As long as we don't get too discouraged or, on the other hand, bumptious, and as long as you over there don't ever get patronizing or 'Told-you-so'-ish, we'll do fine. See, in your country, the electorate tends to get into two fairly solid blocks of opinion behind two fairly constant sets of opinions. That means your government can make decisions more quickly and act more strongly. Now over here, where the government is much more sensitive to public opinion, or to sections of it, before it can do anything it has to know what the general opinion is worked out, the various sections have got to have made up their minds what they think, have got to have a mind to call their own."

"Well, surely they've all had some kind of mind about Britain and Europe?"

"Not at all. Millions of people have come here from Europe, either because they were chucked out, because they were being hunted for their lives, or because they were starving. When they got here, all they wanted to do was to learn American, become citizens of a country that would feed and protect them, shut the door behind them and forget it all."

"Well, that's changed, anyway."

"Sure. We all think about Europe now. But with so many different kinds of Europeans here, British, Jews, Germans, Russians, Swedes, Norwegians, and so on, there are a whole lot of different sympathies and interests. Sometimes these cancel each other out. Then it looks as if the U.S. doesn't care about the problem. On the contrary, nothing may be happening to the outward eye because we care so much."

"But your more stable, intelligent, well-read thousands," I said. "And your State Department personnel. They might have been more interested in what happened over there?"

"You British have heard a lot about American Isolationists, I know," said Bob. "I wonder how much you know of the times when we Americans were told that we didn't understand European affairs, and were advised —oh, very nicely, mind you—to keep out of them?"

"Well," I said. "I'll take your word for it."

"We could go on like this, swopping recriminations, all night," said Bob. "We could go on like this—providing we had a break now and again to look up the State Archives—till the atomic bombs are dropping. Or till the last wheatfields are lying barren. What's the point? If a guy bears in mind the basic young-old relationship between our peoples, all the taunts and the protests, the charges and the counter-charges—well, even my Aunt Fanny, who only reads dime novels, could work 'em out for herself."

I looked out of the window to where the great pinnacles soared up from the mass of mushroom-small tenements and shops, and petered out in a spire or broke off in embattlements against the deep blue New York sky. "Well," I said. "To-morrow, twelve hours from now, I board the boat for home."

"Fine boats, you British build," he said. "Finest in the world. Have you come across much of the admiration we have for British workmanship over here? Whatever we may think of your poets, your politicians and your policemen, we always admire what the Britisher makes with his hands. We know we can depend on it."

"That's where Churchill understood both countries so well," I said. "He didn't ask for help. He knew you don't like being told what you ought to do over here, and he knew the British hate to receive charity. He just asked for the tools—to finish the job."

"Well," said Bob. "I reckon if we put our energy and your tools, our wealth and your experience side by side—and if there's not too much talking—we've got a good chance of seeing some grandchildren."

"Grandchildren or not," I said. "It'd be a tragedy if we can't get together——"

"*Stay* together. We *are* together now."

"If we can't stay together, so much common stock in the two countries, and speaking the same language. By the way," I said, "I'm surprised that people over here don't seem to place as much importance on both countries speaking English as I thought they would."

"There's a reason. In Britain, you're only a few miles from four or five countries where people speak tongues different from each other and different from your own. Over here, if a man lives in the mid-west, say, people speak his tongue for a thousand miles in each direction. So he takes language for granted. It never occurs to him that speaking the same language as some other nation makes much odds. He doesn't know the disadvantages of speaking a different one. No wonder we speak, say, French so badly."

"The French say that nobody speaks French as badly as the English."

"I don't know about that. What I do know is that speaking the same language sometimes strikes me as being a barrier between our two countries. The language hides so many important differences between us. Because a man speaks the same tongue, you kind of expect he'll think the same way, act in the same way, as you do. It hides the pot-holes. You start moving gaily forward with hand outstretched, and next minute you've ricked your ankle. 'Darn it,' you say. Or worse: 'Why in tarnation didn't you say it was there?' Why didn't *he* tell *you*? 'Duplicity,' you say. You both go away, each saying the other's impossible."

"By the way," I said. I got up from my saddle-back chair, and put my coat on. "I know you think English is as much your language as mine: d'you think you could try and stop people over here spelling 'To-night' T-O-N-I-T-E?"

"I'll try," he said, as we walked to the elevator. "But as one English-speaking man to another, do you think that you over there could make up your minds whether it's 'neether' or 'neyether'? I say nothing about your pals Cholomondeley and Dalziel."

"The best people have already made up their minds about neither," I said.

"So they have over here about TONITE," he said. "Good voyage to you, and come back next time. Good night—with a G."

CHAPTER XVII

Americans Are Different

COMPARED with the crossing on the *Marine Panther* the voyage back on the *Queen Elizabeth* was dull and uneventful.

Britain began in New York harbour. Within a few minutes of getting aboard we sat down to lunch in the Tourist Dining-room. "Why is it," said Anthony, "that when you look around here you know at once that you're not on an American ship?"

"Food."

"Clothes."

"Even if we were eating American food and the place was crammed with Americans," said Anthony, "you'd still know it wasn't an American place."

He was right. We wondered why, and discussed various explanations, and then Anthony, we thought, hit on the right one. "It's the way we furnish a restaurant," he said. "The British make it look like a home from home; you know, table-cloths, imitation silver teapot, flowers, sugarbowl and all the rest of it. The Americans just look on the place as somewhere to eat in. They don't clutter up the table with a milk jug; if you want 'cream' in your tea they put it in before they bring it to you. The place is always functional. It has the American look."

"There's another thing about this home-copying business," said Edward. "British restaurants always try and model themselves on a rather up-stage kind of home.

We try and make the waiters look a bit like butlers, and the waitresses like parlour-maids."

"That's why we seem a bit phoney to them."

"Genteel. Genteel is what they least like and least understand about us British. Genteel is what they never are and never could be."

Ten minutes later I stood in the lift which took passengers from the depths of the great ship to the airy top deck. Two young Americans talked in the corner. "All these servants give me the jitters," said the girl. "Me, too," said the man. "All I want's good food and a bunk. Why do they put so much trimming round everything?"

Early on the fifth day we steamed past the Dorset coast. The low, wet, grey raincloud over the bay, the emerald-green of the Isle of Wight rising from the curling spume of the breakers showed us what the Americans see when they first look on Britain. Anthony stood with me on the top deck. "Looks like rain."

"Yes. How many Americans d'you think believe that it's always raining here?"

"Dunno. Most of them, I reckon."

"Somebody told me he'd never seen an umbrella till he came to Britain," said Anthony. "And another chap told me that if I carried one along Fifth Avenue, I'd be recognized for an Englishmen half-a-mile away. D'you think so?"

"If you wore a bowler as well, certainly."

We steamed up into Southampton Water. In what seemed a very short time we were off the ship and cleared by the Customs. Within a few moments of shutting up my bags again I was riding northward across the Hampshire countryside in my father's Austin Ten. It seemed so small it was like jogging along in a buggy. Through the windscreen the hedges, the short green grass, the small, shapely trees, all looked planted. It was like driving through somebody's garden. All seemed quiet, grey and green.

At Ringwood we stopped to get some petrol. "Blimey," said the man at the pump. "You've got plenty of luggage with you."

"Twenty thousand miles since I passed here in September."

He looked at the labels. "America, eh?"

"That's right."

He began to count out the coupons. "Funny you happening to stop here," he said. "My wife's an American."

"Really? How does she like it over here?"

"All right. Finds it a bit damp, y'know, and she misses the coffee. But she says she wouldn't go back to live, even if I upped sticks and went with her."

"You been over there?"

"Twice."

"What d'you think of it?"

"Not too bad. I like the people—they're great. But I didn't like the country. Too much space there, not enough time. Know what I mean?"

"I think so."

"But they're grand people, especially on their own ground. When I go over, my brother-in-law says to me: 'Bert,' he says, 'you don't know the score there over in England. You're back in the Middle Ages. No fly-netting on the windows, no central heating, no paper handkerchiefs, and that B.B.C. Bert, you can't get away from it. You British don't know the score.'"

"What d'you say to that?"

"I just say: 'Put a sock in it, cousin. You're cheesed off because your sister married a Limey.'"

"What does he say?"

"He says: 'You're darned right I am, you son of a

b——!' Then we goes out and has a drink. One night he nearly knocked the block off one poor Yank who said he thought Britain was finished."

Next day I walked round the little village near where I live. The fawn-coloured stone cottages were neat and square, with red fluted tiles and brass knockers on the green-painted doors. Even where they opened almost directly on to the street, there was a line of railings or a low stone wall to claim a strip of privacy. A commonplace scene, neither historical nor romantic. But since I had seen some of the small towns of America, I understood why American troops had raved about it. What looks old to them opens up a new dimension in their minds. It excites them as the new dimension of space excites an Englishman looking down on the mid-west plains from the snow-capped line of the Rockies above Boulder. The American mind moves grandly along in space. The Britisher's, no less grandly along in depth, along the line of his own history.

"Glad to be back home?"

I turned around to find the village schoolmaster. "Yes," I said.

"You liked it over there?"

"Splendid."

The sun came out from behind a cloud. "What's the climate like over there," asked the schoolmaster, loosening his collar a bit.

"There's dozens of climates there," I said. "But I never saw a sky like that—blue and shimmering, with that touch of haze in it. And the sunshine never creeps into your blood through the skin as it's doing just now."

We walked down the High Street, past where a big poster told us that we'd Work or Want, and that we were going to have to Export to Live. "Wonderful thing, Travel," said the schoolmaster.

"Yes," I said. "If everybody I know had five months in America, well, they'd be different people."

"The unofficial visitor," said the schoolmaster. "The man who really wants to travel for the sake of it—not the man who goes on a 'mission,' or——"

"To debate."

"—or to do a deal. The man who goes because he wants to. He's the man that'll change the world."

We walked on in the sunshine. "You going to write a book about the trip?"

"I'd like to," I said. "The place made such a whacking impression on me, I'd like to see if I could make it whack some other people. But I don't know how to get about it."

"Just say what you saw, and what you heard," said the schoolmaster. "Which reminds me. What do they think of us over there nowadays?"

"Well, quite honestly," I said, "I don't think most of them do think much about us. Just as most people here don't spend much time thinking about them."

"That's right," he said. "That's how it is. It's still the few on both sides that do all the thinking, *and* the talking. I wonder why that is?"

"I suppose it's because it's only the few who do the meeting," I said. "If the many met, they'd start thinking—and talking—fast enough. At present they don't get that personal experience of the other man which puts some life into what they read or hear about him. It's the meeting that does it."

"Well, let's meet a few people in that book of yours," he said. "You can leave out the graphs and the statistics."

"Right," I said. "But it's only the next best thing. Ten minutes breathing the air of the other country is worth a dozen books. Especially over there. It's all so different—even the atmosphere seems different. It's that difference which has to be understood."

"Yes," said the schoolmaster. He leaned on his stick and surveyed the village street, the inn, the old roofs and the apple-blossom on the hillside. "After all," he said; "we in England, and the French, and the Germans and the Italians, even the Russians, we've all got one thing in common. We're descended from the men and women who stayed behind. Over in the States they're descended from the folk who moved away. That makes a big difference. That makes a big gap between us, much bigger than this dollar gap they talk about. It's the gap between where man came from and where he's going. If we don't like where he's going, well, we'll only be able to alter it by understanding it first."